Guided Imagery

Guided Imagery

Creative Interventions in Counselling & Psychotherapy

Eric Hall, Carol Hall,
Pamela Stradling and Diane Young

⑤ SAGE Publications
London ● Thousand Oaks ● New Delhi

First published 2006

SAGE Publications Ltd
1 Oliver's Yard
55 City Road
London EC1Y 1SP

SAGE Publications Inc.
2455 Teller Road
Thousand Oaks, California 91320

SAGE Publications India Pvt Ltd
B-42, Panchsheel Enclave
Post Box 4109
New Delhi 110 017

British Library Cataloguing in Publication data

A catalogue record for this book is available
from the British Library

ISBN-10 1-4129-0148-0   ISBN-13 978-1-4129-0148-2
ISBN-10 1-4129-0149-9 (pbk)   ISBN-13 978-1-4129-0149-9 (pbk)

Library of Congress Control Number available

Typeset by C&M Digitals (P) Ltd., Chennai, India
Printed on paper from sustainable resources
Printed in Great Britain by Athenaeum Press, Gateshead

Contents

Acknowledgements

The authors gratefully acknowledge the contributions of the clients, colleagues and students without whom this work would not have been possible.

To the Reader

This book is written with both the experienced and trainee counsellor in mind. There seemed to us a dearth of up-to-date literature on using guided imagery available for therapists who wanted to include imagery work in their repertoire and who were looking for more than just a tool-kit of exercises. This work is based on research with clients, groups and training groups, going back over 30 years.

All of the contributors to the work – clients, students and colleagues – gave their accounts freely and are published here with their knowledge and consent. All have been anonymised.

Introduction

Imagery: the Language of the Soul

O'Connell and O'Connell (1974) coined the term 'psychonauts' to describe devotees of the personal growth movement in the 1960s. At a time when scientists sent astronauts into outer space, psychologists were developing the therapeutic technologies to journey into 'inner space'. Many of these technologies like psychodrama, psychosynthesis and Gestalt psychology broke new ground, but still borrowed heavily from the great literary and spiritual traditions of both East and West (Ferguson, 1983). Developments in counselling theory and practice put the client at the centre of the therapeutic process. Imagery techniques became widely adopted and developed in these new therapies. Talking cures alone were found to be insufficient to access the deeper recesses of clients' experience and stimulate change.

Rogers' (1951) client-centred approach was in the vanguard of helping clients to develop their emotional intelligence, demonstrating how the relationship between the counsellor and client could provide the necessary conditions for emotional and relational growth to occur. Through the experience of working with a fully functioning counsellor, a client might learn to develop their own self-actualising tendency. Person-centred therapy focused on enabling clients to develop a vocabulary of feeling, a language for understanding their emotional self in order to lead more effective lives.

But, to develop spiritual intelligence (Zohar and Marshall, 2000) clients need to learn the language of the soul (imagery) as well as of the heart (feeling and emotion) and we still have some way to go as a therapeutic community to fully understand how to work creatively and confidently within this medium. Zohar and Marshall (2000: 3–4) define spiritual intelligence as,

> . . . The intelligence with which we address and solve problems of meaning and value, the intelligence with which we can place our actions and our lives in a wider, richer, meaning-giving context, the intelligence with which we can assess that one course of action or one life-path is more meaningful than another.

And go on to tell us,

> ... Some anthropologists and neurobiologists argue that it is this longing for
> meaning, and the evolutionary value it confers, that first brought human beings
> out of the trees some two million years ago. The need for meaning, they say,
> gave rise to the symbolic imagination, to the evolution of language, and to the
> extraordinary growth of the human brain.

Our intention in this book is to introduce and discuss a range of techniques and therapeutic interventions which can help clients generate, express and understand their own symbolic, imaginal language, the language of the soul. Theses interventions are briefly introduced below.

Guided Imagery

Working with guided imagery, the counsellor acts as a facilitator or guide and provides the client with an imagery theme to work with, for example, a journey up a mountain. The client describes aloud the internal images that spontaneously emerge. In the guiding role, the counsellor may invite the client to imagine that they are elements in the imagery journey and even set up conversations between them. We provide an example of the beginning and end of such a guided imagery journey here. The client, Bob, had presented himself as a person who was cut off from and had difficulty in expressing feelings.

Counsellor: The theme for this imagery journey is climbing a mountain. It doesn't have to be a mountain you know, just take the first image that comes of being at the foot of a mountain and describe what you see.

Client: Immediately Switzerland, probably the Eiger, [pause] well from one of the lower valleys. A big chunk of rock, with snow on it from about half way up goes to two peaks, one slightly higher than the other. It seems like another world.

Counsellor: How do you feel about going up it?

Client: Well, [laugh] it appeals to me, it's warm and sort of comfortable on the lower slopes, and even a third of the way up it, but after that it changes quite rapidly. I don't know about going to the top; I think that would be quite difficult.

Counsellor: Well have a go, and just describe what happens.

Client: Yes, OK. At the moment all I can see is sort of alpine flowers in the lower slopes and it's very warm there, and I sort of get sticky walking through the summer heat.

And later as the journey draws to a close:

Client: I've reached the start of the slope of the summit . . . it's very, very bright and it's all snow. It's quite crisp.

Counsellor:	Be the snow and see what that's like. 'I am the snow and I . . .
Client:	And I have lain here for quite a time compacting. I'm completely unbroken, but now somebody's walking on me. . . .
Counsellor:	What does it feel like to be the snow?
Client:	Totally unmoving. I feel like a structure, a tense structure which slowly condenses and changes ever so imperceptively. I like it on this mountain. I'm usually in the sun. I shine very white, only I stay hard. Every now and again there are winds whipping against me and the temperature is very cold.
Counsellor:	Be the wind and see what that's like. 'I am the wind and I . . .
Client:	Well, I career through these mountains.
Counsellor:	What does it feel like to be the wind?
Client:	Well, it's nice being the wind. . . . I'm in everywhere; I completely encircle everything. Brush against everything, and I continue, and I continue, and I continue.
Counsellor:	See if you have anything to say to the snow. 'Snow . . .'
Client:	I will make you hard, I will blow against you and pile on you and make you hard.
Counsellor:	Be the snow and reply. 'Snow . . .'.
Client:	Wind, I like being hard, I like you to blow against me [pause] stiffens and toughens me.
Counsellor:	Be the wind and talk back to the snow. 'Snow . . .'.
Client:	Yes. I can pick up cold from you. I can brush up against you and I can be ice cold. I can swoop down different places carrying all your cold. I can change as I go on. I can pick up other things; I can pick up heat and slowly change, but I just want to be cold because cold is the only thing left. It's right for me to be up here.
Counsellor:	Be the snow and reply. 'Wind . . . ', whatever comes into your head.
Client:	Wind [pause and laughter] I thought there . . . [pause]
Counsellor:	What was the thought?
Client:	I was going to say, 'Wind, I love you', but it, I was too embarrassed.
Counsellor:	What was embarrassing?
Client:	To say, 'I love you'.
Counsellor:	OK. Become Bob again and see what you think about what happened.
Client:	[long pause] I thought it was hard. . . . I took such a long time to recognise . . . a feeling of love, or what I was trying to say was love . . . at the end of it. I was sort of caught out almost in a way. I'm still embarrassed about it now.

In the later discussion, what emerged for Bob was an insight into his difficulty in expressing feelings in close relationships and how cut off he felt from his own emotional core. In subsequent weeks, this imagery journey was used as a therapeutic reference point, a sensory reminder of how it felt to express love. Bob and his counsellor felt that this marked an important turning point in helping him to develop self-awareness and the ability to express emotion congruently.

Scripted guided imagery

In this approach to using guided imagery the counsellor or facilitator provides a narrative structure for the imagery journey. The client or group listen and follow the guide's instructions in silence. This technique is used in situations such as a counsellor training group, a personal development group or a therapy group. It may be used with groups of students in schools as part of personal, social and health education and can even be used with children of nursery age (Hall et al., 1990). Guided imagery using a script is normally used in a group setting, but can also prove useful for a client who is unwilling or too anxious to verbalise their imagery aloud.

The group (or individual) undergoing the scripted imagery journey are encouraged to close their eyes, though this is not essential especially with young children. They are first taken through a short relaxation sequence. Then the counsellor or facilitator guides the group or individual through a script such as 'The Rucksack'. This is a helpful introductory script as clients are being asked to pay attention to issues which are at the forefront of their consciousness.

> Imagine that you are walking along a path with a rucksack on your back. . . . What are you wearing? . . . Have a good look around at the scenery and be aware of how you feel . . . What is the weather like? Become aware of the temperature of the air against exposed skin . . . Take a deep breath and take in smells and scents around you. . . . Now have the sense that the rucksack on your back contains all the problems, anxieties and difficulties that face you in your life right now. . . . Be aware of the weight of your rucksack. . . . How do you feel as you walk along the path? . . . What is the surface like? . . . Is it easy or difficult? . . . Is it level, sloping or steep? . . . Now just go where the path takes you. . . . After a while, you come to a place where you can sit and take a rest. . . . Take the rucksack off and be aware of how you feel without it. . . . Then undo the straps and take out the problems, anxieties and difficulties one by one. . . . As you take them out, have a good look and be aware of how you feel . . . Then place each one down before you move on to the next. [long pause] When you have emptied the rucksack, take a good look at them spread out in front of you . . . Then put them back in the rucksack one-by-one and when they are all in, close the rucksack . . . There is place nearby where you know that it will be safe to leave it for a while if you want to. Place it there if you wish and carry on with your walk, knowing that you can always come back for it . . . How are you feeling now as you walk along without the rucksack? . . . Become aware of the weather, the scenery, the sights, and the direction you take. Just allow the imagery to come and go wherever you want to go. . . . [long pause] Now, when it's right for you, let go of the images. . . . Be aware of the room around you. . . . You might want to open your eyes and move your fingers and toes as you gently bring your attention back to the room.

Invariably, a reflective silence follows a scripted imagery journey, even in a large group. After a pause, the guide invites the group to share their experience, usually in pairs or triads. A scripted imagery journey generates an emotionally charged discussion, which is usually regarded to be personally significant in some way. Participants report feeling calm and relaxed after such an experience. Images appear to be highly memorable and often a client or group member will spontaneously refer back to their experience in a later session, which demonstrates the way the imagery keeps on working beyond the initial experience.

Imagery and drawing

We discuss the ways in which drawing images generated can provide a further dimension to the guided and scripted imagery experience. We have found using drawing as an intervention in tandem with the imagery journey to be a particularly potent source of learning. Drawings can provide a visual portfolio which the client can use as a reference point in terms of monitoring their own therapeutic progress.

Working with spontaneously generated imagery

During the flow of conversation, clients will unconsciously produce metaphors and images, which capture the essence of their experience, for example,

> *Client:* Sometimes I get so down I feel like I'm at the bottom of some deep, black pit.

We discuss the ways in which counsellors can:

1   work creatively with client-generated imagery
2   help them to understand the basis of the emotional response
3   transform the response through re-imagining a more desirable state of being.

Each of these imagery-work interventions will be discussed in the following chapters. The relationship between imagery interventions and bodily well-being is also explored and a review of the research evidence on their efficacy in therapeutic contexts provided. We also offer a consideration of the ethical issues posed by the use of imagery techniques in the therapeutic process. We begin, however, with a discussion of the historical and psychological foundations of the use of imagery techniques in therapeutic contexts.

1

Guided Imagery in the Therapeutic Setting: Historical and Psychological Foundations

What lies before us and what lies behind us are small matters compared to what lies within us. When we bring what is within us out into the world, miracles happen.

(Henry Thoreau, 1817–62)

In this chapter we provide an overview of the historical and psychological foundations of guided imagery and how its use was developed in clinical settings. This involves two distinct strands; first, the approaches taken by psychologists in the empirical research tradition of the USA and the UK and second, developments emerging out of the work of psychiatrists and clinicians in continental Europe. We begin with the problems of defining imagery and the related notion of fantasy.

The challenge of definition is increased by the linguistic confusion created between the terms imagery and fantasy. These terms are often used as if they were interchangeable, although to be precise, all fantasy includes imagery, but not all imagery includes fantasy. If we asked you to summon up a memory image of the first school you attended, the memory image would probably not include any conscious elements of fantasy, even though it might be distorted by time. As a term, imagery tends to be used as an over-arching umbrella concept in a broader sense than fantasy and in a definition distilled from several writers refers to:

An internal representation of a perception of the external world, in the absence of that external experience.

Whereas the term fantasy refers to:

A series of spontaneously created internal representations that may be fantastical, bizarre or unlike any previous experience of reality.

Compare the previous example of the memory of the school with the image of a dragon in a suit of armour fighting a monster with three legs.

The second image will probably have more 'fantastic' or imaginal elements in it. Fantasy is used to describe a *sequence of* internal events that do not necessarily seek to represent external reality in any controlled, rational or conscious sense. Fantasy images frequently emerge and flow in forms that are non-linear, altogether different from everyday experience of time and the material world. Perceptions of time may be collapsed or extended and temporal sequences distorted. Some outrageous fantasies may simply be unusual combinations of earlier experience, such as pictures of dragons and suits of armour and we may be simply combining memories of seeing these pictures in a haphazard way. The term imagery is usually construed to be a positive one and teachers will encourage students to use their imagination, which invariably includes elements of imagery. Fantasy, on the other hand, is regarded as inattention and students are told not to daydream. Both guided and scripted imagery may produce elements of fantasy, but we will use the term imagery as it is used more extensively and understood in the therapeutic community.

Fantasy or reality

Although we have been confidently using terms like 'internal' and 'external' experience, the difference between fantasy and reality is not always clear cut. In early psychological experiments, subjects failed to distinguish between an object they were asked to imagine and a picture of the same object projected onto the back of a blank screen (Perky, 1910; Segal and Nathan, 1964). Sometimes we may 'see' a projection of how we wish the external world to be, rather than what is really there. In the case of mistaken identity, for example, we may see the person we were hoping or expecting to see and, realising the mistake, their features actually change in front of us. Similarly, counsellors and clients may distort their perceptions of each other on the basis of expectations, fantasies in just the same way. In Buddhist teaching the practice of mindfulness focuses awareness on illusion which is considered to be the basis of emotional suffering and the practice of meditation encourages the individual to 'see things clearly' (Hall, 1999).

Using the senses

If asked to report an experience of imagery, individuals will often do it using visual terms, a description of what can be 'seen' in the 'mind's eye'. However, imagery can, and often does, involve any or all of the senses: hearing, taste, smell, touch, balance, hot, cold and pain, as well as sight. In our experience, clients describe images using all of the senses, though many will start with and predominately use visual imagery, even though they may be later encouraged to involve other sense data. If imagined conversations are part of the imagery sequence, then these will be experienced as auditory imagery, sometimes coupled with reports of bodily sensations, particularly in relation to feelings (e.g. butterflies in the stomach) and tension in the muscles.

Vividness and forms of imagery

Hume (1912) suggested that images have less 'force and vivacity' than normal 'sensations, passions and emotions'. This may have been the case for Hume, but it is not necessarily true for everyone. Some people inhabit a rich, vivid fantasy world. This may be a form of compensation for an otherwise humdrum existence or even a form of introversion. It is, of course, equally possible to have a rich external life as well as a vivid inner life. It may be that Hume, by foregrounding the importance of his own rational, logical thinking, diminished the force of his own imaginative capacity as a result.

Galton, the nineteenth-century psychologist, tested eminent scientists on their ability to summon up an image of their own breakfast table. Many of them reported experiencing no visual imagery at all (Galton, 1883). Self-report testimony is fraught with difficulties for the researcher. Psychologists have asked subjects to rate the vividness of their imagery, but there is of course no way of comparing these ratings. A person who claims to be experiencing vivid imagery may be having vaguer images than someone who is more modest in their self-rating. In this respect comparisons of the internal experience of individuals are methodological minefields and finally add little to our understanding of the deep subjectivity of the experience.

Despite problems of self-report, it is likely that there are differences in the quality of the imagery that individuals experience. Again, Galton's scientists perhaps might have diminished their more visual, imaginal capacity by an emphasis on the logical, rational and observable description of external phenomena. However, it is interesting that some exceptionally innovative scientific discoveries have been made in a state of dreaming or reverie. Kekule, a nineteenth-century chemist, came to an understanding that organic molecules like benzine are closed rings or loops following a dream of snakes swallowing their tails. Singer, one of the few psychologists to study imagery seriously, reports experiences of rich visual imagery throughout his life, which may explain the motivation for the direction of his research (Singer, 1974).

Forms of imagery that are not our prime concern in a therapeutic context but which may be experienced during a guided imagery episode are:

1   After-imagery. This can be produced by staring at a well-lit object for a period of time and then shifting the gaze to a blank surface. The resultant after-image is probably due to lingering activity in the retina.

2   Eidetic imagery. This is the ability to look at a complex visual scene and then be able to 'see' it in the 'mind's eye' and describe it in fine detail, as if the eye were a camera. This ability is largely limited to children and people living in non-technological societies (Richardson, 1969). Some formally educated adults retain this ability in the form of a photographic memory. Some lucky students are able to 'photograph' pages of notes and reproduce them later under examination conditions.

3   Memory imagery. This is quite simply remembering or recalling in imagination events from the past. Unlike the photographic quality of eidetic imagery, when we try to remember events from the past, for most of us, it tends to be a relatively vaguer experience. It is more the equivalent of an impressionistic landscape or watercolour of a scene rather than a photograph, so dimensions and perspectives might have changed over time.

4   Daydreaming. Daydreaming is a very common activity, though we may feel guilty about it or even deny that we do it. However, daydreaming is not just an indulgence of the idle, but as Singer (1966) suggests, is something we do most of the time, even when performing complex intellectual operations. Paying attention to the thematic content of daydreams may highlight areas of current concern in your life; either through noticing recurrent patterns of behaviour or by illuminating unfulfilled hopes and dreams that remain frustratingly unrealised.

5   Hypnogogic and hypnopompic imagery. These are respectively the images that emerge into consciousness as we fall asleep or wake up. The dream-like qualities of hypnogogic and hypnopompic imagery may also be present during guided imagery.

6   Dreaming. Dreaming appears to be a universal phenomenon but reports concerning the experience of dreaming vary from individual to individual. Some individuals experience guided imagery as being like their dreams or a dream-like state. However, generally waking imagery is understood to be a qualitatively different experience to dream imagery.

7   Hallucinations and perceptual deprivation imagery. If an individual's sensory experience is limited in some way, perhaps as part of a psychological experiment, under torture such as brain-washing, or even performing a monotonous task, then images may be produced spontaneously by the brain. It is as if the nervous system feels the need to produce visual, auditory and tactile hallucinations in order to make up the deficit when access to sensory experience is limited or denied.

Laboratory-based imagery research

In the nineteenth century, the study of mental states was largely done through the process of researcher introspection, involving the investigators reflecting on their subjective experience of internal processes. This culminated at the turn of the century in the work of Tichener, who is reported to have had unusually vivid visual imagery. He argued that all thinking involved forms of visual and auditory imagery. Other writers claimed that, on the contrary, it was possible to experience imageless thought and it may be that these different points of view stem from the different subjective experiences of the investigators.

The study by Galton (1883) in which he compared the visual imagery of scientists, artists, schoolboys and statesmen (all male) demonstrated a paucity of imagery among scientists and vivid, strong visual imagery among artists. The statement from one of Galton's scientists reflects the position of some contemporary analytical philosophers:

> It is really only a figure of speech that I can describe my recollection of a 'mental image' which I can see with the mind's eye.

It is understandable that the period of introspectionism produced considerable discussion of imagery, as it involved the study of mental content. However, following the development of behaviourism in psychology in the first half of the twentieth century, with its insistence on objective, positivist research methods, subjective phenomena such as imagery fell out of favour as an appropriate area of study. This produced a virtual eclipse of the study of imagery in western psychology until the early 1950s.

In the 1950s, academic interest in imagery began to revive. Roe (1951) examined the differences in the imagery of different kinds of scientists. Physiological research demonstrated that imagery could not be ignored, as differences in EEG recordings were thought to reflect qualitative differences in imagery. Short (1953) reported that subjects with persistent alpha brain rhythms tended to be verbal imagers, whereas subjects within the normal responsive alpha range reflected a predominance of visual imagery. A lack of alpha rhythms in subjects was associated with vivid powers of visualisation and may also reflect the relaxed state that invariably accompanies the experience of guided imagery. This was followed by Singer's (1966) review of research into daydreaming, which suggested that daydreaming occurs most of the time, with most people, and even intrudes into complex, directed mental activity.

None of the published research at this time includes any mention of guided imagery or even acknowledges its existence as part of the therapeutic process. The first formal review of work in the area is provided again by Singer as recently as 1974, in his work entitled *Imagery and Daydream Methods in Psychotherapy and Behavior Modification*. This was followed by Mary Watkins' (1976) integration of literary and clinical approaches to what she calls *Waking Dreams*.

Data from the psychiatrists' couch

European psychologists felt less restricted by the methodological constraints imposed by the behaviourists, and interpreted the outcomes of clinical practice using a philosophically driven approach. This work is reviewed by Ellenberger (1970) who traces the origins of their thinking back to the revival of romanticism in the nineteenth century, which produced a renewed interest in the imagination and the nature of the unconscious. This was partly inspired by earlier work on hypnotism by Mesmer (1734–1815), using what he called animal magnetism, and later by Charcot (1825–1893). Under a magnetic sleep (an early term for hypnosis) several patients appeared to change personality, as if a new persona had emerged, which had an existence of its own. This new personality often showed finer qualities than the patient displayed in everyday life. Similarly, improvements in functioning can result from guided imagery and may even reflect aspects of sub-personalities (Rowan, 1990) which find expression through the generation of imagery.

Myers (1885) wrote about the 'mythopoetic function' of the subliminal self, a way of describing the unconscious tendency to weave fantasies. The term 'mythopoetic' was taken up by Watkins (1976) and used as a descriptive term for the process behind the generation of images during guided imagery. Ellenberger (1970) also discusses the work of Flournoy (1854–1920) and Janet (1859–1947). Flournoy examined dreams, daydreaming, somnambulism, hypnosis, possession and delusion. He came to similar conclusions as Myers, that these phenomena were manifestations of the creative function of the unconscious and that they were capable of generating a wisdom and intelligence that was not conventionally displayed by the individual; as well as producing regressive or bizarre images.

Janet combined hypnosis with spiritist procedures such as automatic writing and crystal gazing to generate images from his patients' unconscious. He believed the images produced in this way were manifestations of split-off parts of the personality, which were repressed into the patient's unconscious. Having brought this material into consciousness, Janet then attempted to change or even eradicate the source of the unconscious material. Binet (1857–1911), a contemporary of Janet, employed similar approaches with his patients. He developed a technique for helping them talk to and converse with the visual images that they produced and then related the material produced to the expression of unconscious personalities which might be inhibiting the patient's growth.

The psychoanalytic tradition grew out of Freud's early experience with hypnosis in the late nineteenth century (Breuer and Freud, 1955). He would press his hand on the patient's head to stimulate images which related to the patient's problems. In the case of Lucy R, he offered her the suggestion that images would appear when the pressure on the head was removed. He was soon to move from the direct use of imagery-generating techniques to the more extended form of free association, for which Freud is most widely known. Free association involved the patient keeping the eyes open which to some extent diminished the possibility of generating imagery. The analysis of visual and auditory images still played an important part in the interpretation of dreams and fantasies and the evocation of early memories. Indeed, Freud decided that reports of early memories of female clients which involved seduction by their fathers were in fact products of fantasy.

Jung (1875–1961) has probably had more influence than any other writer in developing an awareness of the importance of the imagination for understanding the unconscious processes of the human mind. Jung went through a period of intense personal analysis, which included experimentation with spontaneous creative activities, such as building sand castles, carving stone, painting mandalas and pictures. He also describes generating visual images and holding conversations with people appearing in his imagination. Jung (1961) describes these activities as 'confrontations with the unconscious' and argues that the process of free association is often used by patients as a means of avoiding important elements of dreams and fantasies. He stressed the importance of staying with the feelings associated with the images so that they could be more thoroughly understood. He argued that civilized life, with its emphasis on conscious, rational thought processes, encourages the individual to be split off from or unaware of their unconscious processes. However, the energy associated with the emotional aspects of these unconscious processes can break free, often with undesirable emotional and behavioural consequences. He suggests that by working with these verbal elements, progress can be made towards the unification of the conscious and unconscious. This he called the 'transcendent function' (Jung, 1960).

Jung encouraged his patients to use some of the techniques that he had experimented with, such as painting and drawing, in order to explore their own imaginations. Again, based on personal experience, he developed the technique of 'active imagination'. Interestingly this process was undertaken by the patient, outside the consulting room. They were encouraged to re-experience aspects of dreams and fantasies and to encounter and confront elements by engaging them in conversation. This process of 'active imagination' was said to permit experience of the unconscious while awake.

During therapy Jung used a non-directive approach to discuss the imagery clients generated. He would ask questions like, 'What occurs to you in relation to that?', 'How do you mean that?', 'Where does that come from?', 'How do you think about it?' (Jung, 1961). This is a mode of questioning similar to Gestalt Therapy developed by Perls (1976). Interpretations emerged of their own accord from the patient's replies and experiential associations.

Jung believed that unconscious aspects of dreams and fantasy serve an important creative function for the individual when brought into consciousness. This contrasts with the impression given by Freud that the unconscious is merely a sink for experiences, feelings, thoughts and infantile desires that have traumatic and unpleasant associations. Jung, by comparison, suggests that by focusing on the images, they become pregnant with meaning, implying a purposive as well as a repressive function of the unconscious. He goes on to suggest that part of the creative function of the psyche is to provide a dynamic psychic equilibrium for underdeveloped or missing parts of the personality. These other parts of the personality may represent aspects of the personality that are no longer a part of the individual's awareness, or they may represent Jung's (1959) 'archetypes', which have developed in the universal history of human beings.

Another important writer, influenced by Jung, was the poet and philosopher Bachélard (1971). He stressed that human imagination has influence that goes beyond direct sensory experience and makes a unique contribution to the subjective interpretation of the phenomenal world and hence, individual perception of materiality. Bachélard uses the term 'valorisation' to describe the way perception is enriched by affective contortions of reality. Imagination not only refigures the images provided by perception, but goes beyond reality and surpasses it.

In a review of Bachélard's work, Kaplan (1972) suggests that the process of poetic reverie is central to Bachélard's ideas on imagination. Reverie is described as a creative daydream, in which the unconscious can confront perceptions of reality, giving the latter unique emotional associations. This process continues during both sleeping and waking, but while awake, the individual becomes aware of their own creative activity. Bachélard considered that the ability to exercise imagination is central to maintaining mental health, and he discusses the work of Desoille (1966), who appears to be the first to use the waking dream as a technique in psychotherapy in the form we advocate here.

Desoille (1938) developed the use of guided imagery as a complete psychotherapeutic system, though previous therapists had used aspects of daydreams, fantasies and imagination in their therapy. Schultz and Luthe (1969) encouraged their patients to engage in extended visual exercises while in a state of deep relaxation which they had induced for themselves. This 'autogenic state' has the advantages of hypnosis, while avoiding excessive dependence on the skills of the therapist. They also incorporated the ideas of Frank (1910) who suggested that the production of hypnogogic visions in a state of relaxation had a directly cathartic effect for the patient allowing them to drain off excessive emotional responses.

Guillary (referred to in Frétigny and Virel, 1968) in his experiments on 'directed reverie' stressed the relationship between disturbing imagery and motor or physiological problems. He suggests that autonomic responses affect both the emotional nature of the images and the individual's neuromuscular functioning. This relationship between emotion, imagery and bodily tension is stressed by the various schools of body therapists, and is reflected in the work of Reich (1949) and Lowen (1975) and reviewed by Totton (2003). The assumption is made that unconscious material is held in patterns of muscular tension and by working directly on the muscular tension, it can be released, often with accompanying vivid visual imagery.

Caslant (1921) had a direct influence on Desoille and made specific use of ascent and descent in imaginary situations. He found that ascending was generally associated with good feelings and descending with bad or

Table 1.1   Desoille's themes for waking-dreams

Purpose	Theme
1 Confronting one's characteristics.	For a man, a sword. For a woman, a vessel or container.
2 Confronting one's more suppressed characteristics.	For both sexes, a descent into the depths of the ocean.
3 Coming to terms with the parent of the opposite sex.	For a man, a descent into a cave to find a witch or a sorceress. For a woman, a descent into a cave to find a wizard or a magician.
4 Coming to terms with the parent of one's own sex.	For a man, a descent into a cave to find a wizard or a magician. For a woman, a descent into a cave to find a witch or a sorceress.
5 Coming to terms with social constraints.	For both sexes, a descent into a cave to find the fabled dragon.
6 Coming to terms with the Oedipal situation.	For both sexes, the castle of sleeping beauty, in a forest.

depressed feelings. An imaginary journey involving ascent or descent might therefore be consciously employed by the therapist to manipulate the generation of emotional states by moving from one level to another.

Desoille, together with Leuner (1969), has probably played the major role in the introduction of guided imagery into psychotherapeutic situations. Desoille's use of 'le rêve éveillé dirigé' is described as early as 1938, and more recently in an extended account (Desoille, 1966). Therapy, for Desoille, consists largely of a series of imagery journeys, which he believes are curative in their own right. Analysis, interpretation and re-education processes are related to the fantasy journey. The themes he employed and their analytic purposes are shown in Table 1.1.

This is a highly interpretative system and firmly located in a western philosophical and literary tradition, which runs contrary to the emphasis we recommend, though Desoille's analytic taxonomy is understandable, given the prevailing ideas of that time.

Frightening images which emerged during the imagery trips were focused on, to try to discover more about them and their associated feelings and emotions. Desoille assumed that this process would reduce the negative affective charge of the images. He developed techniques to help the patient cope with these difficult situations developed during therapy, for example, monsters may be tamed with the power of a magic wand. If the suggestion was made that the magic wand would transform the monster into a real person, it often turned out to be a person close to or important in the patient's life. Another of Desoille's approaches was to ask the patient to imagine being led by the hand by a helpful, friendly guide. The guide, again, often turned out to be a person who was close to or known by the patient.

Desoille elaborated Caslant's (1921) ideas of using ascent and descent in imagery procedures referred to above. He, too, found that descent was associated with negative feelings and often produced frightening images. Ascent was said to be associated with positive feelings and played an important part in the re-education process. He suggested that these feelings develop through an association with the rising and the setting sun and therefore are universally experienced.

A similar but more systematic use of imagery journeys in psychotherapy is that of Leuner (1969). First the patient is relaxed on a couch, using Schultz's autogenic training method. Over time, the patient is introduced to ten standard imagery themes, representing aspects of the patient's inner life. Leuner claims that the first three themes, the meadow, climbing a mountain and following a stream, tend not to produce frightening material. This is not necessarily true in our experience. Leuner claims that other themes, such as the fierce beast, the dark forest and the swamp tend to produce material that is more challenging emotionally for the patient. He provides additional techniques for dealing with difficult situations on a journey. These include:

1   The inner psychic pacemaker, represented by elements that emerge from the fantasy such as a person or an animal. These elements provide support with difficult problems.
2   Confrontation, in which the patient is encouraged to stay with and become more aware of threatening elements in the fantasy.
3   Feeding, which is used when the threatening element is too frightening to confront. By overfeeding, the monster may become less threatening.
4   Reconciliation, which involves making friends with the threatening image.
5   Exhausting and killing the threatening element in the fantasy. Leuner suggests that this is a risky operation since the threatening element could represent an important sub-personality.
6   Magic fluids, which are used for relieving bodily aches and pains.

Leuner (1984) claims that a series of fantasy sessions can provide therapeutic growth in shorter time frames than conventional therapy. Most of his success was with neurotic patients in clinical settings. He has a modified form of his list of themes for children and adolescents (Leuner et al., 1983).

Kretschmer (1969) provides another approach to the use of specific themes as stimuli for encouraging the flow of imagination. He developed the ideas of Happich (1932) who suggested visiting places in the imagination such as a prairie, a mountain, or sitting by a fountain listening to water. Kretschmer stressed the importance of bringing imagery to a higher level of consciousness. He used the term 'exorcism' to describe the process of change that can take place as a result of these experiences.

It appears that most of the early work developing the use of guided imagery in psychotherapy took place in Europe, mainly France, Germany and Italy. A further Italian development lies in the work of Frétigny and Virel (1968). They used the term 'oneirotherapy', from the Greek 'oneiros' meaning dreams, to describe their use of guided imagery and the term 'oneirodrama' to describe their own form of therapy. They also used the hallucinogenic drug LSD to stimulate the production of imagery – a procedure that would be seen as unethical today.

Manuel Moreno (1967), who was brought up in Vienna, but worked professionally in the USA for nearly half a century, probably had more influence on therapeutic and counselling techniques than is generally acknowledged, particularly in relation to the value of role play and role reversal, which he developed into the system we now know as psychodrama. Moreno suggests both techniques as ways of working with images generated by guided imagery.

Psychosynthesis, developed by the Italian psychiatrist Roberto Assagioli, is another approach to personal growth and development that uses imagery as one of its key tools. Assagioli (1965) describes various categories of symbols that represent, he claims, transpersonal experiences and capabilities. These include introversion, light-illumination, fire, development, strengthening-intensification, love, way-path-pilgrimage, mutation-sublimation, rebirth-generation and liberation. These symbols form the basis of a number of techniques using imagery, ranging from visualisation of extremely specific themes to extended imagery journeys similar to those proposed by Desoille and Leuner. Gerard (1967) played an important part in the development of Assagioli's ideas of pyschosynthesis in the USA and stressed the importance of asking clients to identify with elements within the imagery, such as people, animals, natural phenomena and objects.

These techniques involve an exploration of what is happening in the here and now. This emphasis on encouraging clients to describe their imagery experience synchronously is reflected in all the examples we provide of the use of guided imagery. This approach was given important theoretical support in the existential analysis of Binswanger (1946) and developed in psychotherapy by Boss (1963). Working with dreams, the emphasis was seen as 'being there', or 'dasein' rather than trying to understand the content of the dreams as distorted forms of important parts of the psyche. Rather than trying to see through, fathom or decipher dreams, the dreamer should be helped to experience them. They suggested that the dream is a message from and to the dreamer about their chosen mode of being-in-the-world. We argue that the same can be said of the images generated in guided imagery.

It is, however, Fritz Perls (1969, 1973) who has provided the most comprehensive set of therapeutic techniques for understanding here-and-now experience. Perls makes extensive use of imagery generated spontaneously during the therapeutic session, rather than with the use of specific techniques or imagery themes. An important aspect of his use of imagery is to help the client to 'own' their own projections. As in several of the systems described, such as psychosynthesis and Jung's active imag-ination, the client is encouraged to act out the roles of the various ele-ments in dreams and fantasies. Again, the assumption is made that these elements in some way represent denied parts of the personality.

Conflicting polarities within these elements may be identified and the client is encouraged to act out these conflicts and even engage them in conversation or confrontation. An important polarity described by Perls is between 'top-dog' and 'underdog'. The 'top-dog' tends to be the moraliser, emphasising what 'should or ought' to be done, similar to the superego function described by Freud. The 'underdog' or id equivalent tends to be lazy, backsliding and fearful, and generally gives in to less noble motives or drives.

Perls also used imagery to help individuals understand their physical reactions. Clients might be asked to take on the role of 'the clenched fist', 'the knot in the stomach' or 'the tears that were locked away' or whatever vivid images had been produced during the session. These suggestions were derived from the client's accounts, or what could be seen by the ther-apist. Work on these bodily sensations would sometimes produce strong feelings such as an outburst of anger or an episode of deep sobbing.

Gestalt Therapy was developed out of Perls' ideas and places a strong emphasis on present experience, or the 'here-and-now'. The client is encour-aged to use the first person 'I', rather than distancing themselves from the experience by using words such as 'one', 'we', 'he', 'it' and 'people'. The therapist uses a form of questioning which encourages description of pre-sent experience, rather than looking for hidden motives or explanations. The approach is non-interpretive, though the mode of questioning encourages the client to make their own interpretations.

The use of guided imagery, however, is not limited to psychotherapy and counselling. It has played an important part in the personal growth movement that developed in the 1950s and 1960s and continues to the present day. Two influential books from these early days are Schutz's (1967) *Joy* and Stevens' (1971) *Awareness*. Schutz includes an imagery jour-ney of becoming very small and entering and exploring the body, which he may have adapted from Leuner. This is an imagery journey that we have found particularly effective in practice. An important element of Stevens' book is the guidelines he recommends for a facilitator who is using imagery techniques. He stresses the point that the temptation to project personal material should be avoided.

There is now a wealth of literature encouraging personal growth and self-help, many of which include fantasy exercises and mental rehearsal – mainly generating imagery through the use of a script. The same exercises are often included in professional development courses for business, social work, teaching, nursing and so on, where personal development is regarded as an important element of professional training.

The use of imagery in professional contexts

Guided imagery using scripts is sometimes used in schools as part of personal social and health education development (Hall and Hall, 1988; Hall et al., 1990; Hornby et al., 2003). The use of imagery has been used to generate imagination and creativity in subjects such as drama and art, but more recently it has been used as an approach to facilitating self-awareness. Students, including those who have been described as having emotional and behavioural difficulties, seem to take to this activity readily. Teachers who use these techniques report a more relaxed classroom climate, better quality written and spoken contributions in lessons, improved quality of drawing, high memorability of the imagery and help in understanding complex abstract concepts in subjects including science and maths (Hall et al., 1990).

It is common for professional sportsmen and women and their coaches to use imagery to enhance their performance in sport (Porter, 2003). A golfer will visualise the shot from placing the ball on the tee to the exact spot where it lands. Runners will rehearse going through the whole race in the imagination. There are claims that if an athlete has reached a plateau in the performance of a particular skill and further physical practice seems not to be making an impact, then to practise in the imagination can trigger off the desired improvement.

Imagery has been used in medicine and healing over many centuries. Achterberg (1985) describes how shamans, with no precise knowledge of anatomy and physiology, regarded negative imagery, in the form of thoughts and feelings as the cause of symptoms and illness and harnessed powerful forms of imagery to bring the patient back to health. The credulous response to the suggestions of voodoo depends on the imagination of the individual involved and can even result in death if they believe that this will happen. Even in modern medicine the response to placebos confirms that cure can partly depend on the expectations of the sick person. It appears imagery can have a profound effect on the human body depending on the extent that the individual believes in the suggestions that are being made and their ability to engage with the imagery itself.

More recently, guided imagery has been used directly in the area of health and healing. This assumes an important relationship between imagery and what is happening in the body and negative imagery may be the basis of psychosomatic illness. Imagery has been used to ameliorate problems such as headaches and muscular tension and has also been used to work on the symptoms of serious illnesses such as cancer. The psychotherapeutic and educational value of visualisation has been known about and developed for many centuries in the great religious traditions and in other cultures. One form drawn from Christianity is the Meditations of St Ignatius Lyola (Ignatius, 1992). Another example is in the Vajrayan system of Tibetan Buddhism (Blofeld, 1970).

At the time of writing, the Internet produces a prodigious number of sites in response to the key words 'guided imagery'. Many of these are from people selling tapes of imagery journeys using scripts which are designed for healing or general health. There are a substantial number of personal development and interpersonal skills training manuals that include fantasy journeys for individuals or groups. The majority of these applications involve passively listening to a script, rather than the interactive form which we go on to discuss in the next chapter.

2

Guided Imagery in Therapeutic Practice

I have spread my dreams under your feet,
Tread softly because you tread on my dreams

(W.B. Yeats, *Heaven's Embroidered Cloths*)

Counsellors who use guided imagery as part of their therapeutic repertoire need to consider the following issues:

- managing client expectations and assumptions
- clients' preparedness and readiness for the activity
- timing and time implications for generating and working with guided imagery
- the physical setting of the counselling room
- additional equipment, e.g. paper, drawing equipment, clay and so on.

Clients arriving for counselling or psychotherapy will rarely expect to be asked to close their eyes and relax, let alone engage with guided imagery, so careful preparation is essential. Occasionally it would be appropriate for a new client to be asked to engage with imagery work early in therapy though the counsellor needs to be sensitive to the client's expectations, assumptions and stereotypes about what might happen in a counselling session. It would be appropriate where the client has contracted to engage in a desensitisation process, had come for hypnotherapy, or had specifically requested sessions which involved the use of guided imagery. The introduction of a therapeutic intervention which involves imagery is a matter of professional judgement. However, the enthusiastic convert needs to be careful not to assume that what worked well for them in training is likely to work just as well for their clients and to resist the temptation to introduce imagery in every session.

Aside from choosing an appropriate moment to introduce the use of imagery, a key consideration must be how such an intervention can be fitted into the therapeutic hour, as the imagery journey and subsequent processing can take up a considerable proportion of the time. An imagery journey can be successfully included in a 50-minute time period, particularly if the client has been prepared for this in advance, but on occasion a two hour session may be necessary to complete the process. Some imagery interventions can be introduced effectively into time-constrained brief counselling or therapy. Clients may even be more receptive to imagery work that is introduced spontaneously or intuitively in response to images as they emerge and techniques for using this approach are discussed in Chapter 7.

Starting out with a client

If you decide to use imagery work, the idea needs to be broached with the client and a clear explanation offered as to the nature of the process itself. A client may have come because of your reputation for using imagery, but it is much more likely that your client will be naïve about the process. A form of words such as the following might be useful.

> *Counsellor*: I'm going to suggest we use a technique called guided imagery in order to get a clearer understanding of what is going on for you right now. It may seem a little unusual at first, but many people find it useful as a source of learning. Some of the challenges we face don't necessarily have neat or rational explanations and using guided imagery can be a way of helping us access the feelings and emotions related to these events. How do you feel about trying this out? Are you happy to have a go? If at any time you begin to feel uncomfortable or upset, we can stop.

The approach to gaining the client's consent and co-operation needs to be tailored to their intellectual ability, age and emotional readiness. Young or less well-educated people may need a very simple explanation. Intellectuals may need to be offered some type of research evidence that there are positive outcomes from guided imagery and we provide this in later chapters. Most clients are keen to try anything which helps them to resolve the difficult issues they face, as long as they trust the professionalism of the counsellor and are happy to let them be the best judge of the approach taken in therapy. However, reinforce the message that the client is in control by using the following formulation.

> *Counsellor*: If at any time you want to stop for any reason, just open your eyes and the images will go of their own accord. If you would rather not say what is happening at any particular moment, but want to continue with the imagery, just say, 'I don't want to talk about that'.

A client may give a wry smile in the middle of an imagery journey and when asked, 'What was that thought?' will say something to the effect, 'I'd rather not talk about that', but still remain deeply involved in the sequence of images. It is important that the counsellor does not give in to a natural curiosity and press the client for further details.

In our experience, only a minority of clients refuse to engage with guided imagery. They tend be maladaptive perfectionists (Rasmussen,

2004) for whom control and predictability are paramount. Imagery work may feel too open-ended and risky for them to handle. The client's decision must be respected, but the underlying reasons may provide productive material for discussion. For all their organisation and control, clients with this pattern of behaviour still get depressed and anxious, and using an 'out of the box' technique such as guided imagery could provide a potent interruption of this cycle.

If a client consents, it is helpful to develop a vocabulary which guides the client into the process. The first time you try this, the words may sound clumsy, because they are not phrases commonly used. Over time, however, they will become part of your normal repertoire. Counsellors during training should have the opportunity to practise these verbal interventions, so that using the language for the first time in therapy, the client is unlikely to notice any hesitancy or the counsellor experience feelings of performance anxiety.

In terms of formal seating arrangements, an upright easy chair is probably best, as in this position clients can take a relaxed, full breath. Slumping in a bean bag or on a cushion can restrict breathing. Some clients will prefer to lie on the floor if there is space for this. Many counselling rooms only have high backed armchairs and these are usually perfectly adequate. An upright chair makes it difficult for the client to fall asleep and is probably the most comfortable over a period of time. If the client insists on a different position, it is best to go along with them, even though they may seem to be uncomfortable. Given the choice, most clients prefer an easy chair or sofa if they are told that they will be asked to relax. Consideration also needs to be made of any physical disabilities which might influence the way a client needs to sit or lie down.

> *Counsellor*: Make yourself comfortable in the chair. It is probably better to sit upright rather than lean back so that your breathing isn't restricted. There's no reason for us to be disturbed, but you may hear noises in the building or outside on the street, such as people going up and down the stairs and the sound of cars outside. You will find that despite these noises, you will still be able to relax and engage with the imagery. Any noise you hear will help you to relax more deeply.

External disruptions can happen in the quietest environments. If you are working in a busy urban counselling practice, external noise is inevitable. Police and ambulance sirens can be piercing, but if the suggestion is made beforehand that any noise will not be disruptive, but serve as an aid to deeper relaxation, then this will help clients to focus and concentrate their attention inwards. Any disruptions that do occur can be built into the preamble and even into the beginning of the imagery journey, if appropriate. Once the journey is underway, clients rarely appear troubled by extraneous noise. One of the authors had the experience of hearing a clock chime loudly 11 times in the room. At the end of the session, the client reported that although she had heard the chimes, they did not interfere with her experience or concentration.

From the outset, it is helpful to encourage the client to relax, but there is no need to spend too much time over this as the experience of imagery is relaxing in its own right. The counsellor needs to be alert to cues given off by the client in response to the suggestions for relaxation. A tense client may need more time while a highly suggestible client will become relaxed after a sentence or two. Clients can be given the option to either close or open their eyes as it is still possible to experience imagery with the eyes open. This is particularly true if the client is a young child. It is worth checking out if there are any physical problems with keeping their eyes closed for any length of time, such as the use of contact lenses.

> *Counsellor*: To focus your attention inwards, it is probably better to close your eyes, but you don't have to if this makes you feel in any way uncomfortable. Take two deeper breaths and with each out breath, have the sense that you are becoming more relaxed. Now I want you to take the first image that comes of . . .

It can be distracting if the client doesn't want to close their eyes and trains the gaze on the counsellor. However, the counsellor should put aside any possible feelings of unease that this might cause.

The next stage: verbal interventions in guiding clients' imagery

In this section we discuss the types of verbal interventions which can help the client both experience and make sense of their imagery journey and explore the images which emerge for them in detail. These suggestions specifically relate to the form of guided imagery where the client verbalises their imagery as it is being experienced. Fritz Perls (1973) was an early advocate of the types of linguistic interventions we recommend here. We are not suggesting that you have to be a Gestalt therapist to work with a client using guided imagery. Nevertheless, the guidelines offered by the Gestalt approach does offer a model for therapeutic interventions which provide appropriate levels of challenge and yet do not attempt to manipulate or interpret the client's experience in any way. You may find that even following these guidelines it is impossible to be completely neutral in your interventions, as inevitably there will be choices about the direction the client's journey may take. Your tone of voice will convey a great deal, for example, if you were to simply reflect back what the client is saying but with an upward inflection, like a question mark, it could convey the impression that you feel the client is taking the wrong direction. The implied question mark might be very subtle but still have a disproportionately significant impact on the client's experience as a whole.

We provide some basic guidelines for forms of language to use when guiding a client. These guidelines appear simple, but may be experienced as rather more difficult to enact once the dialogue is underway. With practice, however, verbal interventions such as these become more authentic and will be experienced as part of the flow of the interaction.

1   Be sparing in your interventions. At the beginning of an imagery journey, avoid intervening too much. Once the client has begun, it is important to allow them to tell their story at their own pace. Rushing in with too many questions or suggestions will give the sense that the counsellor wants to control the process rather than encourage the client to verbalise their experience. If there is a pause, the client may still be experiencing imagery which is significant to them. Research (Hall et al., 1996) has demonstrated that one of the more difficult skills for counsellors-in-training to master is the ability to tolerate periods of silence. On the other hand, it would be inappropriate to allow a silence to go on for too long as session time is constrained. Careful attention to the client's non-verbal behaviour will provide data on when and how to proceed. The question, 'What's happening now?' can be a useful prompt. Sometimes there may be silence but the client will be communicating non-verbally that an internal process is being experienced. After a pause it can be encouraging to prompt:

Counsellor: What's going on for you right now?

Or:

Counsellor: Can you say what that image was?

2   Avoid 'why?' questions. Questions which begin with the interrogative 'why' may curtail or interrupt the flow of the client's journey. 'Why' questions require explanations of motivation and usually distract from the imagery experience because they require a cognitive focus and rationalisation of experience which runs counter to the imagery experience. The suggestion to avoid 'Why?' often causes consternation for the trainee counsellor who may already be in the habit of using it in practice. The use of a 'Why?' question is usually the prerogative of the more powerful and places the questioner in the role of inquisitor rather than supporter.

How can the counsellor prompt disclosure? Ask questions which require factual answers such as questions beginning with, 'What?', 'How?', 'When?' and 'Where?'. It is possible to ask a 'What' question as if it were a 'Why' question because of the tone of voice that is being used, like asking a child, 'What on earth did you do that for?'. Research on non-verbal communication suggests that the client will be paying more attention to the paralinguistic messages that are being communicated by the counsellor rather than the specific context of the words spoken. It is neither possible nor desirable for the counsellor to eradicate their personality from the therapeutic relationship but they need to work towards what (Owen 1991) refers to as 'clean language'.

3   'What's good about . . . ?' and 'What's bad about . . . ?' These questions can be employed to good effect in tandem. There is a tendency in all of us to glamourise or foreground either the upside or downside to situations in our lives. The means to achieving a balance between these tendencies is to examine both negative and positive aspects of experience. If a client has been talking enthusiastically about an insight arising from an image, try asking if there is a flipside. Here is an example from a client who was talking about his life as a tree.

Client: I have a strong thick trunk. I provide support for other parts of the tree. When there is a strong wind or a gale, I hold everything together. I have been doing this for many years and the foliage and branches have come to rely on me.

Counsellor: Is there anything bad about being strong, providing support and being relied on for such a long time?

Client: I get tired. Sometimes when the wind is blowing strongly, I feel that I am going to snap and break in half.

This intervention changed the tenor of the imagery journey and resulted in a discussion of the client's need to look after himself and also his life script of taking on responsibility for other people. None of this material was either implied or suggested by the counsellor, but emerged simply from putting the question 'what's bad about . . . '. Similarly, a client can be asked to focus on the positive side to a theme which is apparently negative as in the following example.

Client: It's very cold on the top of the mountain and I feel frightened because there is no one with me. There is no one to help me if I get into trouble. It is scary being completely on my own.

Counsellor: What's good about being on your own?

Client: I feel as though I am in control of my life. That's strange. I don't think I have ever had that feeling before. I still feel scared, but I really want to push on.

4   The Assertive 'I'. Assertive use of the personal pronoun 'I' is encouraged in basic training for counsellors and is also important to the process of guiding imagery journeys. Just notice in social interactions how people avoid using the first person. Pronouns such as 'we', 'you', 'one' and 'it' are used to distance the self from responsibility for the statement that is being made. However the counsellor's role is not to import spurious or non-existent rules into language and this in fact may be culturally inappropriate. The point is to enable the clients to develop an awareness of what may lie behind a simple verbal act. Is it good manners or lack of assertiveness – culturally inappropriate or a refusal to own a feeling? The counsellor's role is to offer the challenge and allow the client to explore what emerges for them.

Client: There's a mist coming down and I can't see the path clearly. You get anxious when you don't know where you're going.

Counsellor: Try saying, 'I get anxious when I don't know where I am going.'

A more subtle form of avoidance is using the word 'it' when 'I' is actually meant. The novice counsellor may need to pay particular attention if the client does this.

Client: The path is coming to an end and the side of the mountain is becoming very steep now. It is very scary.
Counsellor: Try saying, 'I feel scared.'

If the suggestion is given to personalise a statement, some clients may find it hard just to get the words out of their mouths. This difficulty could form the basis then further exploration in a later session, if the habit is firmly embedded. Other clients will consistently avoid using 'I' but it is important not to keep reminding them of these lapses, as it can interfere with the flow of expression. The suggestion to use 'I' can be withheld until a potent moment, when it may serve as a key to unlock insight rather than a corrective tool which feels punishing emotionally to the client.

5   How do you feel about ... ? Clients may have a tendency to avoid talking directly about feelings or speak in an emotionally detached, incongruent manner while describing their images, even though the content itself is dramatic. If this is the case, encourage the client to verbalise their feelings as they relate to episodes of the journey itself.

Counsellor: Can you say how you feel about being stuck on the mountain and are unable to go up or down?

6   Tracking and reflecting the client's vocabulary. It is important when guiding to use the exact words provided by the client and not to use analogies, similes or words that appear to the counsellor to have the same meaning as the client. George Kelly's (1955) theory of personal constructs argues that even though we use the same words, they will carry different nuances of meaning for client and counsellor. For example, the word 'reliable' can be a positive construct for one person and a negative construct for another. If, unthinkingly, the counsellor attributes a positive connotation to a word when the client intends a negative and reflects, for example, 'reliable' back as 'safe', but the client meant 'boring', this will prove confusing. In an example given earlier, a client refers to his experience of being a tree with the words 'strong', 'relied on' and 'for a long time'. The identical words and phrases are fed back in the counsellor's response. Adjectives such as 'powerful', 'dependable' and 'endless' may appear to have the same meaning, but there is no guarantee and changing the words may be confusing to the client. During training, beginning counsellors may be warned against 'parotting' when reflecting back a client's train of thought; however in guiding imagery accurate vocabulary training is a core skill.

In order to try to stay with the client's exact vocabulary, one of the writers uses an image of a filing cabinet at the right side of his head. As key words emerge they are filed in the cabinet and pulled out at what intuitively feels to be an appropriate moment. Often for the client to hear the exact words fed back to the by the counsellor can prompt insight into their significance.

Client work: Becoming the image and taking on elements of the fantasy

We refer to specific parts of the imagery as elements and discuss the ways in which these elements can be used as part of the therapeutic process. Any image generated can technically be described as an element, but usually specific images will stand out and have emotional significance for the client.

Client: The river reaches the edge of the cliff and pours over the edge with tremendous power. I am standing there amazed by the power and energy of the waterfall.
Counsellor: In imagination become the waterfall and experience what it's like to have that tremendous power. [pause] Try saying, 'I am the waterfall and I . . .', anything that comes.
Client: I am the waterfall and I feel so powerful, I can sweep everything away in my path. I have so much energy that I find it scary. I feel stronger than anything else around me.

Clients report that making contact with significant elements within the imagery provides them with a source of insight into their own qualities and characteristics such as strength and energy in this case. Focusing on and amplifying these qualities can help them cope in their everyday lives. Often simply by recalling the imagery, the sensations can trigger off the feeling.

Clients who fight shy of more conventional forms of role play appear to find little difficulty with the instruction to become the element. Some clients may refuse, but will continue with the imagery journey itself. We have only had a tiny minority of clients who find this suggestion too difficult a challenge. It seems that once the client has agreed to take part and is engaged with the imagery, they are prepared to go along with even unconventional instructions.

If the client has managed to take on the role of an element, it is then possible to encourage a dialogue between the element and the client.

Counsellor: As the waterfall, see if you have anything to say to Susan [the client]. Perhaps begin by saying, 'Susan . . .' and say anything that comes into your head.
Client: Susan, why are you just sitting there looking weak and pathetic? You can be strong and powerful like me. You don't need to take so much notice of what other people say about you.
Counsellor: Now become Susan and reply. 'Waterfall . . .' Say anything that comes.

The role play can be ended after a single statement or be developed as a conversation between the element and the client. It may even be possible to set up a conversation between two or more elements. A common element which emerges during the progress of a river is for there to be a powerful, fast-flowing waterfall, with a deep, still pool at the bottom. Conversations between the waterfall and the pool can be revealing for the client with, for example, insight into strength with the waterfall and wisdom in the hidden depths of the pool. Choosing when to set up these dialogues is an intuitive judgement on the part of the therapeutic guide and it is important not to over-indulge in asking cleints to take on the role of elements and to allow the flow of the client's own imagery sequence to unfold.

How does the counsellor know which images or elements to work with? Particular images which stand out for the counsellor may prove of little import to the client, but sometimes working with apparently insignificant images can be effective. The choice may have more to do with the counsellor's needs than the client and the counsellor can inadvertently manipulate the client to work with an image that is more helpful to them. It is also important to avoid choosing an element because it worked well with a client in the past, as the significance of each image will be strikingly different. Taking on the role of elements is similar to the Gestalt method of inviting a client to place aspects of their personalities or important people in their lives onto another chair – 'hot seating'. They are asked to confront the person or trait and engage in dialogue as well as switching between roles. This approach will be familiar to Gestalt therapists who use guided imagery.

Magical solutions: Overcoming imaginary blocks

Sometimes a client will reach a point in the imagery sequence where they appear to get physically stuck. It is surprising how real this sensation of 'stuckness' can be for the client. A client journeying up a mountain may come to a steep place and be unable to go up or down. In a situation like this, the counsellor can offer a 'magical solution' as a means of providing the client with a creative or paradoxical means of escape.

Counsellor: Imagine that you have grown wings and can just take off and fly away from the side of the mountain and can land anywhere you want to.

Or:

Counsellor: Build up the sensation that you are becoming lighter. Breathe into the lightness until you can just float to the top of the mountain.

Or:

Counsellor: Take a magic wand out of your pocket and use it to find a way of rescuing yourself.

The sensation of 'stuckness' is a powerful metaphor for the life situations in which many clients find themselves. Escaping from the feeling, if only in imagination, can prove to be a liberating experience and even for the briefest moments provide a glimpse of the power of positive thought. Magic wands, potions, spells, helpful fairies or angels, rings with special powers and invisibility cloaks are only a few of the limitless possibilities. A range of magical solutions was offered by Desoille (1966), though Leuner (1984) argues that these devices should be avoided in order to encourage the development of a more mature ego.

We would suggest that these 'magical' interventions should be used sparingly, as they are, in essence, an intrusion into the client's experience of their imaginal world and might potentially be disruptive. On the other hand, they could prevent the imaginary journey coming to an end prematurely and should be reserved for situations where the client feels blocked from making progress and needs to be shown ways of thinking creatively about problem-solving. Alternatively, the counsellor can simply bring the imagery to an end, as in the example we give later in the section on ending. This alternative needs to be couched in a positive way, so the client does not feel that they have in some way 'failed' or that they leave feeling hopeless and still 'stuck'.

Bringing the client back to the room

Unless the client chooses to end the session themselves, the counsellor usually decides when to bring the imagery journey to a close. There may be a natural ending, but dependent clients will wait for instructions as to when they should stop. Some clients pack so much apparently important material into the first few minutes of an imagery journey that it can be helpful to pause at the first appropriate moment to reflect on the wealth of images that have been generated. Other clients enjoy the relaxed state so much, that they would happily go on beyond the therapeutic hour, but this should be avoided, unless a double session has been booked, as it precludes an opportunity for reflection on the process. A gentle suggestion from the counsellor that it might be a good time to end is usually responded to fairly quickly.

> *Counsellor*: OK, this might be a good moment to bring the imagery to an end. Perhaps take some deeper breaths and begin to **slowly start to come back to the room**. When it is right for you, perhaps **open your eyes** and **come back to the room**. Perhaps move your fingers and toes and if you wish, have a good stretch and a yawn, bringing the sense of relaxation back into the room with you.

If the words printed here in bold are spoken clearly and slowly, they will act as embedded commands which help the client emerge smoothly from a relaxed state (more of this in Chapter 8). Some clients will ignore these suggestions and sit enjoying the relaxed state, which possibly they may not have experienced for some time. There is no need to rush in and break the reverie. We have no experience of a client who was unable to emerge from the relaxed state induced by the imagery. If, however, the client does remain in a trance-like state and seems unwilling to emerge from it, a gentle squeeze on the wrist will usually bring them back to the room. Being unable to bring them out of the imagery is an anxiety expressed by counsellors who use imagery for the first time, but it is not an anxiety shared by clients themselves, who report feeling in control of this process.

Clients are often enthralled by the imagery and lose a sense of time. There can be an experience of collapsed time and a 25-minute imagery journey is experienced as being much shorter. There does not appear to be any evidence about the optimum length for an imagery session and this will remain an intuitive judgement made by the counsellor, as many clients will happily continue for as long as they are allowed.

It is encouraging for both counsellor and client to end a session on a relaxed, happy, energised or positive note. Usually, this is not too difficult to facilitate, as a good proportion of the imagery will fit this category and the ending can be brought about during one of these episodes. However some clients can end up in a difficult imaginary situation and appear to be stuck in it. The following examples come from clients reporting with depression. The first imagined herself dead at the bottom of the ocean and there was no way that she could find to be brought back to life. The second client journeyed down inside a mountain crater and ended up with the mountain on top of her. In both examples the counsellor simply instructed them to withdraw from the imagery. Neither client described the images as damaging and, on the contrary, reported that the experience provided a clear analogy for the experience of depression. Interestingly, both clients reported feeling temporarily less depressed after the imagery work and achieved a greater awareness of and insight into the nature of their depression.

Once the imagery journey is brought to an end, clients need time and space to reflect consciously on how they are feeling and the process more generally. This can bring insight and learning about their ability to relax, their overall psychological state and the quality of their interpersonal relationships. A minority of clients report feeling more tense after the imagery journey. A possible explanation is that the relaxation that accompanies the experience allows them to become aware of just how tense they are for the first time. This insight provides an indication of the need to learn to become more relaxed. An even smaller minority claim that they experience no imagery at all. Gentle probing invariably produces evidence that some degree of imagery was experienced. A counsellor in training reported a total lack of imagery, just the colour black. When encouraged to draw the colour, actually included a deep shade of red, until satisfied that the colour match was exact. The trainee was encouraged to dialogue between the colours red and black and this produced a profound and moving description of her interior life. Clients who persevere despite claiming that they experience difficulty in generating imagery, often go on to develop a vivid imaginal life. Certainly exercising the imagination can improve the imaginal capacity, just like practising any skill, will improve performance over time.

Reflecting on and learning from the experience

After bringing the journey to a natural conclusion, the next stage is to ask the client to discuss the meaning of the experience. Unprompted, clients may use words to the effect, 'I've been talking about myself, haven't I?'. This is probably best followed by an open question such as, 'Can you say some more about that?'. If this acknowledgement isn't forthcoming, another possible intervention is to ask, 'Is there anything like that in your life right now?'.

Occasionally a client will introduce a new, potent image while talking about the imagery journey. It may be appropriate to invite the client to close their eyes once more and explore this new image, particularly if the earlier imagery journey had been brief.

For even the most experienced counsellor, it is an ongoing temptation to interpret the client's experience and to provide neat explanations of what the imagery 'means'. Some therapists would take this further and offer a theoretical justification for the interpretative method in terms of sub-personalities (Rowan, 1990). Interpretations related to sub-personalities or other forms of interpretation may be appropriate in some contexts and we will discuss this issue in more detail in Chapter 4. In our experience, even if clients don't understand precisely what lies behind the images at first, they are hungry for the opportunity to discuss them with someone who cares.

If no sense or apparent meaning emerges for these images, the client needs to be reassured that it can take time for the significance to unfold and the client can be asked to reflect on the meaning of the imagery as homework. During an imagery journey down a river, one client went into the water and had the experience of large creatures brushing against her body. She was frustrated that she could get no sense of the meaning of this image. She returned the following week and said, 'I now know exactly what the strange creatures in the river meant to me.' The discussion then developed around this new insight. If the counsellor were to have provided an interpretation of the image, then the possibility of self-generated insight and learning would have been lost. Clients may even experience memorable dreams that they relate back to imagery generated in a previous session. Counsellor-generated interpretations or labelling of these experiences encourages a premature closure to reflection and can inhibit learning. There certainly does appear to be a strong sleeper effect that allows the meaning of imagery to percolate into awareness long after the session has ended. Clients can recall vividly images that emerged many sessions earlier and often report that recalling the image has been helpful to them at difficult, stressful moments in their lives.

3

Themes in Dialogic Guided Imagery

The themes included here are those we have found particularly potent for clients and trainee counsellors over many years, but we would encourage counsellors to be creative in building their own bank of imagery themes. We suggest, for example, that technology provides a fresh source of themes relevant to a client's experience.

There are three main sources of themes for the counsellor to use in one-to-one sessions:

- existing psychological literature and new themes such as those involving technologies
- themes that the counsellor creates to meet the specific needs of the client
- themes which emerge out of images spontaneously generated from client–counsellor dialogue.

An idea for an imagery theme might emerge out of an intuition based on prior knowledge of the client's psychological state and an assessment of their readiness to explore their situation more deeply. On the other hand, the client can be offered a choice of themes and invited to decide intuitively what is right for them at that moment.

Leuner's (1984) imagery themes have had a substantial impact on practice although his influence in the field remains largely unacknowledged. Leuner recommends a specific thematic sequence for therapeutic use. Some themes he believes to be 'introductory' and less likely to induce threatening imagery, and others more 'advanced', requiring an experienced guide with advanced training in the use and management of guided imagery in therapeutic practice. However, our case experience suggests that any theme can be either 'introductory' or 'advanced', depending on the experiential associations made by the client to the specific theme and the skill of the counsellor. The first three themes we discuss are the introductory journeys suggested by Leuner: the Meadow, the River and the Mountain. We treat them as independent themes, whereas Leuner would combine more than one at a time as part of a therapeutic intervention. We would certainly advise against introducing more than one imagery theme in the therapeutic hour, given the need for preparation, process and reflection.

With each of the themes we discuss, clients should be prepared using a brief relaxation procedure such as the suggestions we offered earlier. Once a client has become familiar with this routine, the need for an extended relaxation procedure becomes redundant. It is important to prepare the client psychologically, but the strong association built up between experiencing internal imagery and a feeling of relaxation, enables clients to relax quickly and effectively.

Theme: The Meadow

Using this theme, the client is simply invited to explore a meadow in their imagination. Depending on geographical, cultural, educational or linguistic background, the counsellor may need to explain the meaning of the term or help the client relate the idea of a meadow to their own experience.

> *Counsellor*: I'd like you to summon up an image of being in a meadow. It doesn't have to be a meadow you know or that you have visited. Just go along with the first image that comes into your mind and as the image becomes more real to you, actually see yourself in the meadow. Now describe aloud to me what you can see. Be in the meadow. And now if you can, don't just see yourself in the image. Be there, looking through your own eyes at what you can see around you.

The final suggestion, to have the sense that you are looking through your own eyes is vital, as it appears to make an important contribution to the vividness of the imagery which emerges. Observing yourself in the image in a voyeuristic manner becomes a means of remaining distant from the experience and taking on the role of spectator rather than protagonist. Clients will often report that they feel like spectators in their own lives, so it is helpful to offer the suggestion early on in the process. If a client begins with a phrase such as, 'I can see myself walking through the long grass . . . ', then make the suggestion, 'Try saying, I am walking through the long grass and I can see . . . '.

The Meadow is offered as a relatively pleasant theme, to enable clients to become accustomed to the idea of the imagery journey and Leuner encouraged therapists to begin and end an imagery journey in a meadow because of its relaxing and peaceful associations. Generally, the meadow as a theme appears to produce a less dramatic sequence of images, but to repeat our earlier caveat, in our experience, all themes have the potential to feel either safe or threatening to a client and it is what is projected onto and into the image which determines its characteristics. If the client's imagery journey strays from the confines of the meadow, there is no reason to discourage this. In fact, going beyond a boundary, real or imaginary, could relate to an important issue for the client. If the client does venture beyond the meadow, it may be helpful to suggest returning before ending the journey and asking the client to describe the feelings of being both inside and outside the boundary, may produce interesting material for reflection.

Theme: Exploring a river from its source in the mountains, down to the sea or ocean

Rivers (and water more generally) are particularly potent themes because of the parallel association of the river's journey from its beginning to final union with the sea and the human life span. Rivers are universal symbols which speak to us from literary and religious traditions around the world and so readily strike a chord with everyone. The theme involves clients at a deep but relatively safe emotional level. A number of clients in fact have reported that for them the theme acts as an imaginal representation of their life journey, from childhood to adulthood, though of course each client will bring their own meaning to the experience.

To introduce this theme after the appropriate relaxation, the counsellor can offer the prompt:

Counsellor: I want you to imagine that you are in the place where a river begins its journey from its source down to the sea or ocean. It doesn't have to be a place you know; it might be real or imaginary. Just be at the place where you know the river begins and take a good look around you. . . .

'It doesn't have to be a place you know,' is an important reminder. Sometimes the client will recall a real place they are familiar with and continue with a literal description of their memories. This can inhibit the flow of creative imagery and also seems to preclude the attachment of emotional responses to images as they emerge. Nevertheless, some clients start with specific memories and quickly shift into producing more creative imagery. Once the client has begun, there is little point in interrupting and insisting they start again.

For many clients the river begins its life as a flowing, clear stream, which contrasts with the slow moving and often polluted or cloudy river below. Waterfalls are common, often cascading into a deep pool, and both elements, the waterfall and the pool, can be productive images to work with, perhaps comparing the energy and movement of the waterfall with the calm depths of the pool. Rocks can be threatening elements or obsta-cles on the journey, though not always so, and fish can be mysterious, benign or threatening. A creative intervention for an adventurous client is to suggest that there will be no problem with breathing under water and to invite the client to swim beneath the surface. They can then be invited to go down the waterfall or flow through the rapids and see what happens. Clients who manage this, report a strong sense of release or catharsis, like an emotional bungee jump, where they have taken a risk and survived. Another potent intervention is to ask the client to become the river where it meets the sea or ocean and to merge with it. With no irony intended, several of our clients have reported oceanic feelings of interconnectedness which they regard as spiritually significant and this feeling of cosmic connection stayed with them for some time after the session had ended. Zohar and Marshall (2000) would argue that this is a manifestation of our innate spiritual intelligence helping the fractured self to heal using imagery as a tool.

The journey of a river theme has consistently been a rich source of spiritual insight for clients who become deeply involved in the journey itself and later report that they experienced the images as clear representations of important aspects of their life journey. Seeing the process as a whole provides an opportunity for a detached perspective which is sometimes missing for clients caught up in feelings of hopelessness or lack of meaning in their lives. During a river journey, one client reported that as the river she felt in full flood and was scared that she might burst over her banks. She was invited to allow that to happen. She recounted that as the river she flowed over all the surrounding countryside and that experience created the most wonderful orgasmic feeling and provided her with an insight into the ways she prevented herself from letting go and the unlooked for consequences of her self-control.

Theme: Climbing a Mountain

Counsellor: I want you to imagine that you are about to begin a journey up a mountain. It doesn't have to be a mountain you have visited; it can be real or imagined. You are at the bottom of the mountain. Be aware of how you feel about going on this journey. Don't observe yourself in the imagery, actually be there, looking at the scene through your own eyes. Now, as you set off up the mountain, be aware of what you are wearing. Feel the textures of your clothes against your skin. Are you carrying anything on your back? What is the weather like? Smell the air around you and listen for any sounds you can hear. Describe aloud what is happening . . .

Again, some clients may choose a mountain they are familiar with and this can potentially limit the creative possibilities of the imagery but others will create the mountain for themselves in imagination. They may be influenced by mythical or story book mountains such as in classical mythology or popular literature. The mountains may vary from low, round hills to steep, precipitous snow-covered mountain ranges. There may be easy paths or sometimes the way is so steep that climbing equipment is needed. You might invite the client to become the mountain and to engage the walker in conversation and vice versa. Clients often ascribe powerful qualities to the mountain such as strength, stability, dependability, immortality and disciplined persistence, which may be traits that the client themselves has felt out of contact with for some time. Reconnecting with these forgotten, denied or buried aspects can be extremely affirming and clients can come to understand that these characteristics are once again available to them.

It may be that on occasion, clients fail to reach the summit or get stuck on a steep cliff or gully. If this happens, it may be necessary to offer a magical solution to find a way out of the perceived impasse. A creative way of bringing the journey to a safe conclusion is to encourage the client to imagine that they can take off and fly wherever they want to. There may be a wind or air stream on the mountain top and the wind can be a useful element to enter in imagination and dialogue with the mountain. If the client is able to identify with the wind, try the suggestion 'and now blow wherever you want to'.

Another creative intervention is to invite the client to find a way of exploring inside the mountain, particularly if the main part of the journey appeared uneventful or naturalistic. This will demand a shift to a more creative set of images. One client discovered that her mountain was a volcano and was able to 'become' the volcano and to erupt. Afterwards, she described this as an extraordinarily cathartic experience, a release of pent-up tension, having led a very controlled life for many years.

Leuner (1984) suggests that the height of the mountain and the difficulty or ease with which it can be climbed is indicative of the individual's ambition, aspirations and even general approach to life. We have had examples from our casework which appear to support this hypothesis, but there are always exceptions. Climbing the mountain does appear to have elements of struggle, which clients quite naturally identify with. One client recalled three years later:

> I remember the mountain clearly. At the start I had no idea what to take on the journey so I chose water and a rope. It was a slow, painful, and lonely walk up the mountain path. The path was winding with side paths which were dead ends. On the way up I met some people who were not at all helpful to me on my journey. The landscape was bare, hard and desolate. I remember that I went round and round – not straight up. Straight up would have been far too steep and difficult. It is my journey through life. I am still climbing. I know that you have to go round and round and overcome many obstacles before reaching the top. The imagery helped me to understand my life.

Theme: Exploring a House

Exploring a house can be left as an open theme or with a specific emphasis on going up into the attic or down into the cellar. If Caslant (1921) is correct, that descent is more likely to produce negative feelings, going down into the cellar should be avoided for clients who feel particularly depressed or hopeless. Caslant's caveat has to be carefully set against the possibility that it can also be beneficial for us to experience negative feelings and confront them positively. The counsellor will need to exercise both professional judgement and intuition about whether it is the right moment for the client to confront their depression rather than to stay trapped in it, which appears to be the experience of many depressed clients.

As with other themes, it is helpful to have a preparation phase before engaging with the central theme and entering the house. This can be done by asking the client to be outside the house and describe the exterior appearance and report the feelings that this generates. The client can then be prompted to describe how they feel at the thought of entering the house itself.

Counsellor: I would like you to build up the sense that you are going to go into a house to explore the attic. It doesn't have to be a house you know. Take the first image that comes to you of a house and standing outside, describe the exterior in as much detail as you can . . .

The interior of clients' houses will range from luxuriously furnished to being very bare or spartan. Some will be small with no windows and others are stylish mansions with ornate gardens. Clients may express anxiety about going up to the attic or down into the cellar, indicating an uncertainty about what they might find there. It is, however, useful to encourage them to work with the feeling of unease, gently working with their resistance, rather than insisting. It is not uncommon to find a forgotten childhood toy in the attic and this can be a rich image to focus on. Freud (1900) argued that the image of a house is a representation of the client's personality or psychological inner life. We argue that all elements from any theme are also, in some sense, reflections of the personality. Leuner (1984) when working with children and adolescents used the people in the house as a way of working on patterns of family relationships and dynamics. In our experience, however, the houses of the adults we have worked with tend to be empty of people and the creative work involves exploring any objects discovered within the house, which might include childhood toys or memorabilia.

Theme: Entering and Exploring your own Body

This theme encourages the client- to become very small and to enter and explore their physical body. This is one of Leuner's so-called advanced themes and an extended example of its use is described by Schutz (1967) as an 'into the Body Fantasy', in which the individual becomes very tiny and, in imagination, enters and explores her or his own body. In the same way as in the river and mountain themes, a person with a knowledge of the physiology of the body might provide a literal anatomical description and one client actually digested themselves in the first few sentences! On the other hand, we have the experience of working with doctors who had no problem with entering into this journey in a creative and fanciful way, producing an image of the body that doesn't appear in any medical text-books, despite their knowledge of the body's anatomy. If literalism is a real stumbling block for a client, the counsellor might suggest that the small person wears a protective suit.

> Counsellor: I want you to imagine that you are becoming very, very small; so small that you could enter your own body. Describe what is happening as you become very small and how you feel about this happening . . . [pause]. Now choose a way or place to enter your body and describe aloud what is happening. . . . Just go along with where the journey takes you.

An alternative is to invite the client to imagine that they are about to enter their body through the mouth and are standing on their own tongue. This can prove an anxious moment on the journey, as the client can perceive the drop down into the throat as frightening. It may be necessary to invite the client to invent a magical solution in order to circumvent the fear or even invite them to find an alternative place to enter the body in safety. Once past this hurdle, it becomes easier to relax into the imagery and the descent down the throat has been reported as a liberating experience for some.

Once the client has entered the body, the fantasy journey continues in a whole range of directions. A common route is to visit the heart and brain. If a client visits both, it can prove helpful to explore the relationship between the two in greater detail by setting up a conversation between them. This may seem something of a cliché but the difference between the stereotypically emotional heart and the rational brain is an enduring and meaningful metaphor across cultures. This split often raises important issues for clients with maladaptive perfectionist tendencies, who have a need to ensure that they have a rational explanation for everything they do. We have, however, had the experience of clients who report stone-like hearts and fuzzy, cotton-wool-like brains and these counter-stereotypical descriptions can prove a rich source of personal insight.

Sometimes an exploration of the body reveals that parts of the body are experienced as diseased, ill, damaged or even tied up in knots. One of the writers has developed the technique of entering the body accompanied by a maintenance person to sort out potential physical problems, particularly if a health problem has been identified beforehand. An alternative is to suggest that there is an army of willing workers who live in the body and who can be sent anywhere to carry out essential maintenance or repair work. There are many creative techniques which use imagery to assist physical and psychological healing and we discuss these in more detail in Chapter 8 and review the research evidence for their effectiveness.

Theme: Searching for and Finding a Rosebush

The image of a rosebush is suggested by Assagioli (1965) and further developed for use in psychosynthesis by Ferrucci (1982). Stevens (1971) uses it in working with personal development groups. From our own educational and therapeutic work we have found two interventions with this theme particularly useful. First, after a period of relaxation, to simply invite the client to become a rosebush and to explore what life is like as the rosebush; secondly, to go on a journey to find a rosebush and then to become the rosebush itself. We would prefer the second approach, as the journey allows the client to become more deeply involved in the process of discovery before they begin to explore the central image of the rose-bush. It has been suggested that the image of a rose enables us to connect with our sexuality or sexual identity. This may be the case with some clients but it is unlikely to hold true for all and counsellors should steer clear of jumping to hasty or easy interpretations.

In the following example, the client recalls her guided imagery experience from four years previously. It is another example of the high level of the memorability of imagery, when accompanied by strong emotional associations.

Client: In the sequence I imagined myself to be a dark red rose growing in a garden. The rose was set apart by itself. The rose was fully mature, velvety with many petals open and perfumed. The brown hard thorns on the stem were particularly meaningful to me. There were no new thorns only old ones. There was a gardener present in the fantasy. I remember that I allowed the gardener to remove most of the thorns. To do this he wore thick leather gloves and simply and gently smoothed the thorns off. They just fell away. The image of the rose clearly reflected my old defences and hurts which I had held onto over the years. I still recall the sequence today as being instrumental to my healing and integration process.

Theme: Going Through a Gate or Door

Opening gates or doors can provide metaphoric insights into new and exciting challenges and possibilities. It is as if the client can literally now see a goal to work towards, where previously there had only been an impenetrable wall. One of our clients reported that her wall had no door, no way out, and that this echoed her experience of depression. Working on this theme enabled her to envision a means of escape from her cycle of hopelessness and helplessness.

> *Counsellor*:   I would like you to imagine that you are approaching a wall and that there is a door or a gate in the wall. It might be a wall inside a building or outside in the open air – the first wall that comes into your head. At the moment you are some distance away from the wall and I want you to describe what is happening and how you feel as you walk closer to the wall and describe your experience as you approach the gate or door.

From this point it is useful to encourage the client to describe both the wall and the gate in detail and to build up to actually walking through it. Some clients will stride through confidently while others have difficulty in finding a way through, with locks that can't be opened or latches and handles that won't move because of rust or great age. It can be helpful to invite the client to take on the role of the obstacle and to set up a dialogue between the client and the element. Out of this dialogue can emerge greater understanding or insight into the very essence of the client's self-blocking mechanisms. From this understanding the next step is to envisage a future without blocks, and set goals to move forward.

Another approach is to use a door into a building or a house and a further variation is to have several doors and to invite the client to look through them into the space beyond. Going through a gate invariably leads into a garden and this provides a rich source of imagery. From our own casework, a high proportion of the gardens are idealised, with beautiful flowers and it is considered a delightful place to be for the client, in comparison with the other side of the wall, the space they usually inhabit. With one client the garden had an area that was wild and untended and a tiger lurked in the undergrowth. The client's own interpretation was that this represented his own strong id-like urges which he kept ruthlessly suppressed and away from his otherwise well-ordered life.

Theme: The Waterfall

We discussed the importance of waterfalls as cathartic images in relation to the journey down a river. The image of a waterfall in itself can be used creatively for clients who find themselves at turning points, crossroads or decision times in their lives. The natural energy contained in the flowing water seems to be capable of inspiring and revitalising even the most depressed. The following example we developed for more passive clients who describe feeling stuck in a negative emotional or depressed state arising out of their inability to make important life choices. Despite being

directive at times, there is still the opportunity of free flowing interaction
between the counsellor and the client.

Counsellor: I want you to imagine a waterfall. Take the first image that comes.
It doesn't have to be a place you have been; it can be real or imaginary. Take a good look at the waterfall and the scenery that sur-
rounds it. Describe aloud what you see and feel right now. [pause]

And then:

Counsellor: Build up the sense that you know there is a cave behind the waterfall. A place that you are sure is safe for you. Find a way into the
cave. What is it like? What is the temperature? Feel the texture of
the walls. Listen to the sounds. How do you feel about being in this
cave? Is there anything you want to do here?

And then:

Counsellor: Now have the sense that it is safe for you to stand in the waterfall
itself. You can come to no harm. Find a way of standing in the
waterfall and describe what happens and how you feel.

And finally:

Counsellor: Try walking out from under the waterfall, into the open air and the
river beyond. It is as if you can walk on the water itself. Describe what
happens and see how you feel as you emerge from the waterfall.

Here are some extracts from a client who suffered from anxiety and
reported feeling highly stressed after a demanding period at work.
Initially she found it difficult to enter the flow of the waterfall, but finally
managed it and recounted the following:

Client: It's so refreshing, quite cool but not too cold. My skin is tingling. I am
going to go further in. Oh! That's lovely.

At this point the counsellor chose to reinforce these positive feelings in
order to provide a trigger for relaxation and energy during other periods
of stress.

Counsellor: Just enjoy the water rushing over you. Feel the power of the water
passing through every part of your body from head to foot. Let the
water touch and heal all those anxieties. Let the tiredness go into
the stream. The water will heal and energise you. Can you feel that?

A long silence followed. The client's face wore a blissful expression and
she later commented:

Client: It's heaven in here, I could stay for ever.
Counsellor: Enjoy the feelings a little longer. There is no rush, just relax.

The client remained silent for some minutes and later when the counsellor brought the journey to a close said:

Client: *I am trying to hold onto every detail. I don't want to leave it.*

The counsellor then offered the reinforcing suggestion that the client had the power to recreate the feeling at will.

Counsellor: Can you file the memory of the waterfall somewhere safe in your mind? Then you can revisit it whenever you want. It belongs to you.
Client: Yes it's a clear picture in my mind. I feel unbelievably refreshed; quite exhilarated in fact. I felt so safe, free, not a care in the world.

The following written account comes from a client who wanted to record the inner conflicts and struggle symbolised by the journey. Notice how at first the client doesn't find it easy to enter the waterfall despite its aesthetic appeal.

Client: At first glance, the waterfall is all and its splendour is a magnificent sight. By no means lacking in lustre, its indisputable beauty is evident and I for one find it both stunning and captivating. Focusing on the waterfall I feel drawn to come, stand under the waters and experience all that's in the offing; refreshment, restoration, cleansing, purification, renewal and transformation. I feel the buzz of excitement anticipating all of this. I want to run forward with urgency in my stride and allow myself to be saturated, to allow myself to be soaked.

I know, however, that I cannot take another step. For as much as I feel a certain warmth, the waterfall also conjures up feelings of anger, fear and despair. Why would the waterfall want me to stand under its waters? What's the catch? I come tainted, unclean and with paralysing disbelief that it will indeed do everything it offers. How can I stand? Does that not in itself make a mockery of its greatness?

If I do muster up the courage to go on, if I do chance my arm, what then? The waterfall is unpredictable. On the one hand it can flow in a gentle manner and then in the flicker of an eye can change its mood becoming violent, ferocious, irritated and out of control.

I feel angry that on the one hand it is able to use its power and might to heal you and on the other hand destroy. I am fearful that the waterfall can smite you and wipe you out without warning, without sentiment and there is nothing that can be done to change this, leaving you abandoned, stripped, cold and empty. Who would want that?

As these conflicting emotions collide within, I know that the waterfall is too risky. Potentially it could ruin me. What's the point in that?

This key existential question, 'What's the point in that?' was a pivotal moment in the therapeutic process, when she found the courage to face her own inner doubts and fears about annihilation.

Another example comes from a client who reported feeling depressed and anxious. As she entered the waterfall she said:

Client: I am turning the waterfall into slurry.
Counsellor: Can you walk along a bit to a clean stretch of water?
Client: Yes and I am also turning that into slurry.

This could be read as a negative experience and potentially counter-productive to the therapeutic process, but in a later session, the image of turning the waterfall into slurry was used constructively to explore the client's learned resistance to positive change in her life. She went on to use the image as a tool to deal with stressful moments as she found the image relaxing. She later reported that the water was slowly becoming clearer as the slurry dissipated. This demonstrates how learning which emerges out of the imagery can be used as a measure of therapeutic progress by the client as well as the counsellor. The ability to detach from here-and-now feelings is an important aspect of self-awareness. The client began to use the image as a barometer of her own emotional well-being. Generally waterfalls prove to be healing images for clients, particularly those who report high levels of stress and tension. Conjuring up the image of a waterfall can be a relaxing, but paradoxically active strategy, to employ when needing to calm an over-active brain or hyper-aroused nervous system.

Theme: The Volcano

The image of a volcano can be emotive as it carries associations of unpre-dictable and spectacular eruptions which can be seen as metaphors for violent outbursts of feeling. For example, we might describe someone as having volcanic anger. In the following extract, the client admits to own-ing deeply repressed feelings of anger, but feels unable to get in touch with them in a safe environment; hence the counsellor's suggestion to use the volcano as a way of being more aware of and in touch with these feel-ings and as a way of understanding and controlling them more effectively.

Counsellor: Now you are feeling relaxed I want you to imagine that you are at the foot of a volcano. It doesn't have to be a volcano you are famil-iar with – it can be real or imaginary. Build up the feeling that you are going to climb to the top and look down inside the crater. Are you ready to begin?
Client: Yes. I am walking slowly up the path. I am a bit nervous that I may fall off. But I am getting calmer as I go on, almost floating in fact.
Counsellor: Take a good look around and tell me what you see.

Client:	It's grey on the ground – no plants at all. The path is getting steep. Oh, and now I see smoke. I can smell it like barbecue smoke!
Counsellor:	What's happening now?
Client:	I think I may be getting near the rim. . . . Yes I feel the heat. I see sparks of fire. I feel a bit scared.
Counsellor:	Is there a place where you can stand that looks safe and where you can carefully take a peep over the top of the rim?
Client:	Yes, there is a place over there. I am going now. I am looking over the top. I can see into the heart of the volcano. Oh, it's red and very hot.
Counsellor:	How do you feel looking into the heart of the volcano?
Client:	I feel very small . . . a bit naughty . . . as if I am not allowed to look . . .
Counsellor:	Would you like to say anything to the heart of the volcano?
Client:	Yes. What are you doing? Are you going to explode or what?
Counsellor:	Now, become the heart of the volcano and see what it replies. As the volcano, what do you think of this person standing on your rim?
Client:	I am the heart and I am just bubbling away nicely. Don't be scared of me. You seem to quite like me.
Counsellor:	What would you like to say back to the heart of the volcano?

At this point, the client took control of the dialogue without further prompting from the counsellor.

Client:	I feel I want to be your friend.
Heart of the volcano:	I don't mind you being here. Don't be frightened of me. I am quite all right.
Client:	OK. Then let me see what you can do!
Heart of the volcano:	I will make a small eruption . . .

The client then began to puff and blow and made several banging noises with her hands.

Client:	Bang, bang, bang!
Counsellor:	Can you describe what's happening?
Client:	It's raining fire and rocks – hot rocks – deadly red dust is flying – massive shoals of fire, but I am really enjoying it. I am excited.

The client continued to walk energetically up and down the room clapping and making banging noises.

Client:	I feel good.
Counsellor:	OK, perhaps allow the volcano to subside now. As you watch, check out how you are feeling as the images gradually fade. Take one last look and perhaps say goodbye to the volcano.
Client:	Yes. Goodbye and thank you volcano. I feel very energised, very released and good.
Counsellor:	When you are ready just breathe a little more deeply, stay relaxed and when it is right for you, bring your attention back into the room.

After this episode, the client reported feeling less angry and tense. At home she continues to find a creative physical release from pent up angry feelings by becoming the volcano and clapping, puffing and blowing her anger away.

Theme: My Computer

Clients disclosing maladaptive perfectionist tendencies were initially resistant to engaging with guided imagery. However, an image which did engage them proved to be that of the computer. We offer variations on this theme, beginning with the image of an emotional hard disk, which emerged out of an earlier session with the client. Satir (1972) describes the computer-type personality as coldly aggressive, out of touch with feelings of anger, and presenting in a cold impenetrable, perfectionist manner.

Counsellor: Can you imagine what your emotional hard disk is like?
Client: Yes.
Counsellor: Would you like to explore it a little?
Client: Yes, mmmm. There's a lot of anger and resentment in there.
Counsellor: What do you think might happen if the disk was full?
Client: I am stressed out at even the thought of it. I think I would just fall to bits if it was full.
Counsellor: That sounds very stressful. Shall we have a go at downloading some of the feelings contained in there?
Client: Yes, I know I need to.

The client went on to explore some of the feelings in the disk and the implications of greater self-disclosure; an idea he had been unable to engage with up to that point in therapy.

The next extract involves an image of a computer operating system, which was generated by a client with low self-esteem and with a very pessimistic mind set. His life experience seemed to live up to his gloomy, negative view of himself. Using this image helped him become more aware of the destructive effect of his negative scripts. Notice how the counsellor prompts more than usual in this example, because of the client's reluctance to verbalise experience. This form of verbal withholding is associated with Satir's (1972) computer-type.

Counsellor: You said you have a PC. I want you to imagine you are switching it on now.
Client: Yes, I'm doing it now.
Counsellor: OK. Sometimes you can see a glimpse of the computer system code flashing up. Can you visualise that?
Client: Yes.
Counsellor: Can you imagine that the scripts tucked away at the back of your mind could work like a computer operating system? They control

	what you do and what you think. Perhaps we can use the image of
	the computer to help you find some of these. Then you may want
	to make some changes to your system.
Client:	That's cool, I like that.

The client went on to explore the unhelpful patterns he had created and how they were problematic for him. The use of an image which had meaning for him meant that he was able to engage with his self-defeating behaviours. Conventional therapeutic approaches had failed to produce this emotional engagement.

Professional clients consistently reported the computer-related imagery as helpful. Images drawn from technology, particularly computers or computer operating systems, appear to permit them to enter an imaginary world which is safe and familiar because it offers elements of control, logic and organisation. For professional clients, images taken from the technologies they work with on a daily basis will be meaningful in ways that at present we can only imagine. Today's technology will provide therapists with the classical imagery themes of tomorrow.

Having successfully engaged with imagery using this somewhat mechanical, rational mode, clients have been able to move onto themes drawn from the natural world. A development of this technological theme would be to take the client through a series of windows or menus or split screen and so on.

A variation we have used to good effect with clients with seasonal affective disorder (SAD) is to invite them to design their own mental screen saver. They are invited to choose a journey to find a place in the sun or in intense light. A client invariably chooses a sunny, warm landscape with vivid, blue skies or sea. The client is encouraged to tune into the positive warmth of the imagery and amplify their positive feelings and replay the image when they wake up in the morning or fall asleep at night.

Counsellor:	Just imagine the warmth and light of the scene flowing through
	your whole mind and body. Notice how the light lifts your mood
	and intensifies your sense of well-being. Now can you hold the
	scene in imagination and remember, you can call it up just as you
	would a screen saver on your computer. You can recall this scene
	and the feelings that go with it whenever you want to visit your
	special place.

Homework

Many of our clients tell us how they use key images from their journeys for some time after the experience in the counselling session. In almost all of the following examples, clients spontaneously decided to do this as homework, and without being prompted, later spontaneously reporting their progress.

Client: I turn the temperature down in my shower and imagine that I'm in the centre of a beautiful waterfall. I feel energised and de-stressed by that healing experience and I do it every day.

Client: I call up the image of sitting in my special haven to get me through the day.

Client: When I am being criticised, I deflect the harsh words as if they were arrows using the golden shield that I hold in front of me.

Client: Before an important meeting, I bring up the image of being presented with a prize, which gives me the confidence to present my papers without fear.

Client: The image of falling out of the boat was shocking at first, but now it's a life preserver for me. I use it every day when the going gets tough.

Client: Leaving my anxieties behind in a stone in the counselling room has been great. When I am anxious and stressed I just imagine the image of the stone in a safe place and I feel held and calm.

Client: Now I have an image for the feelings, they are not so powerful and I'm not frightened.

Client: Now when I have the feeling of a weight on my chest, I can use the image of just shrinking it and I feel more in control.

After an initial experience of using guided imagery, clients may ask to repeat the experience and clients can be given the opportunity of working with a series of themes. Some even ask for a contract that involves extensive use of imagery work, having being recommended by a friend who feels the imagery journeys have worked for them. This chapter has discussed the use of guided imagery themes in counselling. The counsellor acts as a guide offering minimal suggestions, designed to encourage the client to experience the images as fully as possible, without interpretation or direction from the counsellor. In the next chapter, we discuss the counsellor–client relationship in the guiding process.

4

Counsellor Perspectives on Managing the Client–Counsellor Relationship

Love seeketh not Itself to please
Nor for itself hath any care,
But for another gives its ease,
And builds a Heaven in Hell's despair.

(William Blake, *The Clod and the Pebble*)

Interactive or dialogic imagery journeys by their very nature require the facilitation and support of a guide. We wouldn't usually encourage clients to do this themselves, except when they are using the images as 'homework' for positive reinforcement or to recall positive images at times of pressure or stress. It is possible to self-guide, but with our own experiments, the mind has a tendency to wander off the theme and the process becomes more akin to a daydream than an imagery journey. An important exception to this is the use of a specific image or series of images designed as part of a self-healing process for an illness or injury, as we describe in a later chapter.

The importance of relationship is diminished when the imagery is gener-ated by a therapist on tape or disk, but even in this form the client will respond emotionally to the voice in terms of gender, accent, pitch, speed and so on. Commercial recordings are by nature generic – one size has to fit all. Even though we can buy self-help tapes, there is really no substitute for a living, breathing, responding guide. Therapist-led bespoke guided imagery is the Saville Row of therapy, designed and built around the experience of the client focusing on developing the client's self-awareness and personal autonomy. We go on to discuss the prerequisites of the relationship between the client and the guide for successful therapeutic interventions.

Trust

Trust is a complex, dynamic element of the social–emotional bond created between counsellor and client. Levels of trust will be affected by both interpersonal and intrapersonal factors. What does a client look for in a guide? Someone with experience, knowledge, expertise – someone who conveys confidence and security and looks as though they know how to handle anything that comes up. In short, they want a guide they can trust. Client trust is fundamental to the effectiveness of the therapeutic process. A high level of trust and affiliation is essential if the client is to give themselves wholeheartedly to the guided imagery exercise. In order to risk the uncertainty of the imagery journey, the client needs to trust that the counsellor will always be at their side, both metaphorically and literally.

Some clients tend to supply images that are memories of earlier life, like a tree in their garden or the house they grew up in. The temptation is to describe the memory image rather than engage in a freer flow of creative images. This may show a lack of trust in themselves rather than the therapist and point to an underlying fear of what might emerge if they were to loosen control. If a client insists on staying on a naturalistic level, simply producing memory images, then this can be discussed with them afterwards, but this must to be done in a non-judgemental way.

Building trust by avoiding manipulation

Let's assume the imagery journey is underway. The client is likely to be in a relaxed and suggestible state. Imagery is labile, fluid and easily affected by suggestions made by the counsellor. Every intervention is bound to have an impact, subtle or not so subtle, on the imagery that is produced, so the possibility of manipulation is strong. In fact, we would argue that every intervention the counsellor makes is potentially manipulative in the sense that it has the power to change or redirect the flow of the client's images. The skill is to reduce this effect to an absolute minimum. We would be willing to guarantee that two different therapeutically orientated therapists guiding the same client with the same theme would end up facilitating quite a different imagery journey because of the contrasting interventions and interpretations offered. One possibility is to limit interventions and to offer only minimal encouragement, such as, 'Do go on', 'Can you say more about that?' and 'Where would you like to go now?'. More probing questions can be left to the post journey phase, with prompts such as, 'What did the imagery mean for you?'. However, this would be missing the opportunity for more creative interventions, such as taking on the roles of the elements and dialoguing between them. By avoiding this active guiding role, the counsellor may unthinkingly permit clients to stay heavily defended or in avoidant positions.

Choosing an image

A decision that the guide will need to make relates to which images to choose to work on in more depth with a client. In Chapter 2 we gave the example of a journey up the mountain which gave the choice of working with the image of the mountain itself or a stone on its path. It is likely that any image has the potential to yield psychological insight, but it is also likely that counsellors will make a decision based on professional knowledge of, and relationship with, the client. A client will generate a substantial number of images during any one imagery journey. Any image or element the guide feels attracted to exploring further with the client, needs a mental check to see whose needs are being met by the exploration.

Usually specific images do stand out as key elements. A monster in a cave; a predatory fish in a river or ocean; a waterfall in a river; a secret box in an attic; a broken branch on a tree; a beautiful plant in a garden, are all examples of images that emerge as central in the imagery sequence. Just as an artist painting a picture skilfully draws the eye inward to the central motif of the work, so a client may unconsciously present a powerfully evocative image which inexorably draws the attention of both speaker and listener. There may be a strong emotional and non-verbal reaction to the appearance of the image, which provides a clue regarding the significance to the client. Finally the choice of which element to work with will remain an intuitive one. Although the counsellor is making a choice on behalf of the client in the selection of an element, if the guidelines suggested in Chapter 2 are followed, the counsellor will not interfere with the client's interpretation of the element.

Parallel imagery: the counsellor's experience

As the client experiences the generation of images in real time, it is likely that the counsellor will, synchronously, experience images that are being triggered by the client's narrative. However, it is highly unlikely that the two sets of images will be identical or that the emotional response will be of the same intensity or nature. The parallel journey taking place in the counsellor's imagination may be vivid and generate learning for the counsellor but it is important that the counsellor brackets off these images although they might later form material for a supervision session. Very occasionally it may be appropriate to share parallel imagery with a client, if the self-disclosure would in some way either enhance the trust in the relationship or the client's understanding of their own experience.

Any parallel imagery experienced by the guide opens up the possibility of manipulation, if disclosed or not, rather like the teacher who has the 'right answer' in mind and waits until the student dutifully reproduces it. For example:

Counsellor: No, the river isn't deep and slow. It's flowing very fast with fierce rapids. Just look more carefully and you will begin to see it.

Such an obvious manipulation is crass, but it can be done in more subtle ways, for example, when the guide inserts words or phrases that weren't actually used by the client, but instead describes their own reactions.

Client:	The side of the mountain is becoming very steep now and there is a drop of several thousand feet below.
Counsellor:	How do you feel about this very frightening situation?
Client:	I don't feel frightened, just excited. I can see a wide path and it's perfectly safe.

Just by inserting the word, 'frightening', the counsellor not only disrupts the client's flow, but also adds an incongruent emotional dimension into the dialogue. Some clients will not feel assertive enough to correct or disagree with the counsellor and passively adopt the words in order to please them. In Chapter 2 we discussed how specific words can carry very different meanings (Kelly, 1955). The word 'scary' can mean frightening for one person, while carrying the connotation of excitement for another.

Finally, the guide needs to be alert to any urge to introduce aspects of parallel imagery and, more importantly, avoid any subtle cues which could possibly affect the course of the client's journey. If feelings of disappointment come up about the direction the client's journey takes, the guide should acknowledge this to themselves and perhaps raise it later in supervision. These feelings might signal either performance anxiety or frustration that the client isn't doing the counsellor's work for them.

Detached involvement: An advanced counsellor skill

It is important that the counsellor doesn't try to blot out or suppress these parallel experiences, whether they are visual, auditory, kinaesthetic or olfactory, because this takes emotional energy and attention away from the client. What is required is a shift in attention. A parallel flow of imagery generated internally by the counsellor can be relaxing and this relaxed state can induce intuitive interventions which may not emerge if the guide is feeling tense or anxious. Imagine a split screen on a computer. It is perfectly possible to concentrate on one screen while the other stays at the outer edge of awareness.

Similarly it is important to avoid being overly drawn into the client's narrative and to lose contact with the task of guiding. Counsellors in training who observe clients being guided often report being so caught up in the client's imagery that their concentration wanders away from the counsellor's interventions. The skilful guide is able to stay absolutely attentive to the client's narrative, but not get lost in it, in order to offer the most potent interventions. A useful notion to describe this process is 'detached involvement', which is contradictory, but is the paradox which lies at the very heart of the guiding process and involves a state of relaxed concentration which is similar to that experienced during meditation.

Thus there are at least four important processes occurring simultaneously for the guide during an imagery journey:

- careful listening to the narrative
- awareness of possible interventions
- simultaneous parallel imagery journey and emotional responses experienced by the guide
- attention to the non-verbal messages from the client.

Maintaining a relaxed state of detached involvement is probably the optimal way to function effectively within these modes simultaneously.

A distraction from this detached involvement can occur if the opportunity to make a powerful intervention is missed because the client is in full flow and it would have been intrusive to interrupt. We have found that the narcissistic impulse can result in the urge to squeeze in the intervention at the very next opportunity. This would probably be for the guide's benefit alone and we would recommend that if the moment passes, so should the impulse. Mentally rehearsing what you would like to say, as any trainee knows, can distract attention from fresh elements of the imagery which emerge. A similar narcissistic distraction can be the urge to interpret the content of the client's imagery, an issue we will discuss later.

Stevens (1971) provides a neat summary of the pitfalls to avoid when guiding an imagery journey. His recommendations were for personal development group facilitators and groups in general, but he also related them to guiding imagery journeys. He describes the ways in which a person's experience can be unintentionally disrespected by the guide in the following ways:

- Judging. This can be conveyed both verbally and non-verbally.
- Helping. This often takes place when the client is experiencing what appears to be negative feelings and the counsellor encourages the client to avoid these feelings rather than confront them. Encouraging this avoidance may be meeting the needs of the counsellor rather than the client.
- Shoulds. The same applies to the use of 'shoulds' where the counsellor is telling clients what they ought to be experiencing.
- Explaining. This involves the use of theories, causes and reasons for experience and includes interpretation, which we discuss in the next section.

All these ways of devaluing the client's experience will be a distraction from a direct awareness of the experience itself and reduce potential for learning and growth.

Against interpretation

Throughout we have stressed the pitfalls associated with counsellors 'interpreting' the client's phenomenal world. The process of counselling is designed to re-engage the client with their expertise in self-management. Personal autonomy cannot be achieved unless the client learns the art of developing a critical or meta-analytical perspective on their own phenomenal world. Our emphasis has been to encourage a non-interpretative stance in relation to the images generated and to invite the client to interpret their imagery and relate these interpretations to behaviour patterns in their everyday life.

There is a strong tradition in psychotherapy for the therapist to interpret the client's images and dreams, particularly in the system of psychoanalysis and the developments from psychoanalysis (Freud, 1900). The process of interpretation implies that the images are, in some way, acting as a metaphor for conscious and unconscious psychological processes that reflect aspects of that person. This seems likely to be true, but most systems of interpretation are based on clinical experience and open to distortion according to the theoretical orientation of the clinician. Even some of the systems that suggest that the counsellor should allow the client to interpret their own imagery have implicit forms of interpretation contained within the model. Jung (1961) argues that the only person who can meaningfully make an interpretation is the person who experiences the image or dream. However, his archetypal images do provide a template of interpretation of dream elements. In psychosynthesis a similar recommendation is made and yet to state that an image represents a part of Assagioli's map of consciousness is an act of interpretation in its own right. The paradoxical effect of arguing that the 'map' is not the truth, which is prevalent in psychosynthesis, makes the interpretations even more credible.

The urge to interpret on the part of the therapist can be very strong and potentially related to the unconscious need for power and control in the counsellor–client relationship. We would guess that most counsellors and psychotherapists will do this internally even if they remain silent. As long as the impulse is noted and resisted, they will be less likely to contaminate the client's psychological space. We raise this issue under the heading of the client–counsellor relationship because the act of interpretation is making a clear statement about the balance of power in the relationship. It gives the counsellor power because it implies that the counsellor understands the client's experience better than the client does themselves. In some cases, the client will be desperate for the counsellor to interpret their imagery and indeed many other aspects of what they bring to the therapeutic hour. The experience of prolonged psychological distress is likely to have brought the client to such a dependant state. The act of interpretation reinforces this state of unhealthy dependency and therefore is not to be encouraged.

In a state of psychological dependency the client is likely to be in a suggestible state and an interpretation by the counsellor is likely to be seized upon as if it were a diagnosis which might provide a cure. This is similar to the way individuals take on board the scores from standardised personality tests, tarot and astrology readings and the pronouncements of charismatic speakers. In Transactional Analysis this would be described as child to parent and clients are giving up the possibility of drawing conclusions and learning for themselves about the issues they face. They are reluctant to accept, or wish to stay in denial of, the existential truth that life is in a continual state of flux and change. This state of suffering is caused by the need to cling to the illusion of non-change which Buddhists call dukkha.

Some writers (Rowan, 1983) suggest that it is helpful to offer interpretations but sparingly. Unfortunately, the sparing use of interpretation is likely to have even greater impact than regular use, but this does not mean that it should never be done. A client may ask for an interpretation. One way of responding to this is to share your view, but stress that it is not necessarily 'true'. Begin a statement with words such as, 'My guess is . . . ', or 'My impression is . . . ', or 'My sense is . . . ' and discuss with the client the extent to which the guide can ever fully understand what the client is experiencing.

Taking a calculated risk

Superficially, the notion of taking risks appears to encourage the guide to experiment with the client in a way that could have negative consequences, possibly even aggravating the client's distressed state. The client may be coming to a steep part of a journey up a mountain and is scared to go on. Should you encourage them to continue on the journey? They might meet a frightening monster in a cave. Should you ask them to confront the monster or even take on the role of the threatening image?

In our experience possible interventions pop up continuously and occasionally the thought of making a particular intervention is accompanied by a frisson of what could be described as a mixture of excitement and anxiety. A possible explanation of this feeling is the anticipation that the intervention will encourage the emergence of serious issues that will require considerable skill to handle. This underestimates the extent to which the client remains in control of the process, in spite of the relaxed state induced by the imagery journey. The relaxed state, in fact, gives permission for the relaxation of inappropriate or dysfunctional levels of psychological defensiveness and provides the opportunity to disclose material that may not have been shared with the counsellor. We gave the example in the previous chapter of a client imagining being a river in full flood and anxious that she might overflow her banks. Inviting her to do so was an example of an intervention which carried an intrinsic element of risk. Learning to face risks is a prerequisite for growth.

Taking a calculated risk is the counselling equivalent of what Joyce (1984) calls 'dynamic disequilibrium'. Joyce discusses the process of learning and personal growth in terms of needing to make sense and meaning out of confusion. Becoming the monster or the threatening image tends to reduce its emotional charge and also helps the client to understand who or what the monster represents. The client may even make friends with the threatening image or come to realise that the image represents an important aspect of their own personality. The opportunity to generate imagery and develop explanations of it provides the client with a safe learning environment rather than within the 'real' world which for them may be the source of much of their distress.

In conclusion

The role of the guide is to introduce clients to the use of guided imagery as part of the natural rhythm of the therapeutic hour. As guides become more experienced, interventions emerge spontaneously as a result of deep listening and the client responds without any sense that this is not a thoroughly normal part of a conversation. Interventions can take the form of:

- narrative direction
- prompts for further self-disclosure
- probes in relation to emotional states
- dialogic engagement with and between elements in the imagery.

With practice it is as if both partners in the relationship become enveloped in a subtly flowing energy field, akin to a light hypnotic trance, which is broken when the guide brings the journey to an end or the client decides to stop. The nature of the psychological engagement involved in the relationship is beautifully described in Buber's (1947) classic book, *I and Thou*, which discusses the difference between treating another person as if they were a thing, an 'I – it' relationship and treating them as a person, an 'I – thou' relationship. It is the 'I – thou' relationship that the counsellor should be aiming for – a mutuality founded and nurtured for the client's well-being. If you have the sense that you are treating the client as an object when you practise these techniques for the first time, this is merely a phase of skills development. Once you have honed your skill, these 'techniques' will become a natural part of your repertoire of creative therapeutic interventions.

5

Generating Guided Imagery Using Scripts

Without my journey
And without the spring
I would have missed this dawn.

Shiki (1856–1902)

In this chapter we draw a clear distinction between dialogic or interactive guided imagery and a pre-scripted multi-sensory imagery narrative, read aloud by the counsellor to the client or group. For the client, the first mode is by its nature a public, active process: the second a more private, passive one. In the first, interactive dialogic mode, the counsellor works face-to-face with a client and chooses a theme based on an intuitive or in-the-moment judgement about the developmental or emotional needs of the client. The client recounts their experience aloud in real time and the counsellor uses interventions or prompts to ask the client to expand upon or engage with key elements of the imagery which emerge. It is out of this interactive, dialogic process of exploration that insight and learning can occur.

In the second, the use of pre-scripted narratives, the counsellor or facilitator reads a script aloud to the client or group who remain silent as they experience the imagery in imagination. Such fantasy scripts are applied and researched widely in educational settings with individuals and groups (Hall et al., 1990). Their use is not confined to therapy alone and in fact teachers, sports psychologists, life coaches, executive trainers, all use versions of the technique to harness the power of the imagination to enhance learning or skills development. However, just because the pre-scripted narrative technique lends itself particularly well to the training group context, does not mean that the potential therapeutic benefits should be ignored in the counsellor–client dyad.

In the counselling session, the use of a pre-prepared script is probably a good starting point for a client who may be anxious, shy or introverted because the script is read to them and they aren't being called upon to respond out loud or in public. It remains essentially a private experience. Far less of a demand is being made on the client to self-disclose as the content of the client's imagery is not being revealed to the counsellor in an ongoing way. The client can choose what and how much to reveal during the processing of the experience. Here is a simple example of a script:

Script: A walk along the seashore

Take two deep breaths and allow your body to relax . . . Just let the tension go . . . And now I want you to imagine that you are on the seashore . . . It doesn't have to be a place you know or have visited. It can be an imaginary place . . . Take a good look around you . . . What can you see? . . . Is it a rocky beach or a sandy shore line? . . . What is the sea like? . . . Is it rough or calm? . . . Are there other people around? . . . Become aware of the weather, hot or cold, rainy or dry? . . . Feel the temperature on your skin . . . Is there any wind? . . . Now listen to the sound of the sea . . . Are there any other sounds you can hear around you? . . . Notice the scents and smells of the sea . . . Feel the surface you are sitting or standing on . . . How do you feel about being here by the sea? . . . Now, in imagination, set off to look for a special shell . . . Look along the shore or in rock pools . . . As you look, none of the shells seem quite right . . . perhaps broken or dull . . . Can you see other things in the pools? . . . Now just along the shore you can see the sun glinting in a pool . . . In the pool you will find your special shell . . . Make your way towards it . . . Pick it up and take a good look at it . . . What is the shape like? . . . Is it coloured or plain? . . . Feel the texture of the shell and inhale its aroma . . . How do you feel about holding your special shell? . . . [longer pause] Now put your shell somewhere safe and slowly walk away from the seashore . . . Remember your shell will always be in that safe place if you want to go back and look at it again . . . Now build up the sense that you are letting the images go and when it is right for you, breathe a little deeper and begin to come back to the room . . . But don't rush from the sense of being relaxed.

This is an introductory script and in our experience people of all ages perceive this as pleasurable. However, on occasion, the seashore may bring up negative emotions or traumatic memories, because of a childhood experience or personal association.

As with guided imagery in a one-to-one situation, the client can be encouraged to talk about or draw one or more elements of the imagery arising from the script and with the drawing in front of them, the clients may be encouraged to talk in more depth about their experience. The same counsellor techniques we discussed in relation to verbal processing of the dialogic form of guided imagery also apply to the processing of a scripted imagery experience.

In the example of being by the seashore, the narrative line has been kept to the minimum. The intention is to allow the client maximum opportunity to develop their own imaginal responses. For example, if the counsellor were to suggest that the client feel the warm sun on their face when they already had an image of a cold, windy day, the need to change the imagery or to summon up the energy to ignore the suggestion is likely to disrupt the process to some extent. It is helpful to remind the client in the preamble to the session, that all responses to the counsellor's script are acceptable. However, if the counsellor has chosen a particular script to suit a dilemma that the client is facing, it is worth suggesting that the client might also find it beneficial to go along with the narrative line provided.

Script: A safe place

Another way to support a client who is anxious about engaging in a free flow of imagery is to focus specifically on the issue of safety. This can be done using a short sequence in which the client is invited to create a safe place.

> Take a few deep breaths and have the sense of relaxing with each out breath . . . It might be helpful to close your eyes, but if you prefer, you can keep them open . . . Imagine that you can have all the resources you want to create your safe place . . . Is this place large or small? . . . Inside or outside? . . . What sort of textures can you feel around you in this safe place? . . . Have a good look round and be aware of what you can see. . . . Is it furnished? . . . What are you doing right now in this safe place? . . . Take a deep breath and really take in the smells . . . Now spend a few moments to take in what it is like to be here in your safe place . . . [longer pause] Now, when it is right for you, begin to come back to the room . . . Perhaps breathe a little more deeply, open your eyes when you are ready, and gently come back into the room.

This is a useful script to follow with a drawing of the safe place and we will discuss how to introduce drawing in Chapter 6. A client can employ this image as an emotional refuge or self-affirmation during periods of stress or anxiety.

Feedback from the client will determine their willingness to engage further with imagery scripts. It may be possible to move on to a potentially more potent theme. The following script is intended for clients who may be experiencing a feeling of 'stuckness' in their lives, or for whom decision-making is seen as problematic. It can also prompt deep reflection and insight into the general existential theme of change and its consequences.

Script: Bird in a cage

> I would like you to summon up an image of a bird in a cage . . . Take the first image that comes to you . . . What is the bird like? . . . What sort of cage is it in? . . . How do you feel about this bird in this cage? . . . In imagination now, become the bird in the cage and experience what it feels like to be the bird . . . Don't see yourself there. Look through your own eyes as the bird . . . How does it feel right now to be the bird in this cage? . . . What is your cage made of and what sort of texture is it? . . . How do you feel about your cage? . . . How much space for you is there in the cage? . . . Is it large or small? . . . Are there any other birds or are you the only one? . . . Now become the cage and experience what it is like to be the cage . . . How do you feel about the bird that you contain? . . . Now, in imagination, notice if there is anything that you would like to say to the bird . . . Say, 'bird . . . ' and just go along with anything that comes . . . [longer pause]. Now become the bird again and see how you feel about what the cage has said. . . . Reply to the cage saying, 'cage . . . ' Anything that comes . . . [longer pause] Now, in imagination, if you want to, see if you can find a way of getting out of the cage . . . If you manage

to get out just go anywhere you like . . . Just allow the images to emerge . . . Go wherever you wish to go . . . [longer pause] Now, in imagination, see if you can find a way to get back to the cage . . . If you manage it, see how you feel about being back in your cage . . . When it is right for you, allow the images to fade and the feelings to subside and begin to come back gently to the room.

Each client generates a unique range of responses to this script. The birds may be large or small, plain or exotic. Some are in a large aviary with other birds and some hemmed in by themselves. Some birds are literally unable to leave the cage or perhaps restricted to the room which housed the cage, while others roam far and wide. Some birds feel glad to be back in the cage because of dangers outside, while others deeply resent returning. Some are simply not willing to return to captivity and remain free. Superficial or hasty interpretations of these elements of the imagery should be avoided and we would reaffirm our recommendation that the interpretation is left to the client through a neutral form of questioning by the counsellor. A tight cage may feel snug and comforting for one bird and claustrophobic for another. The counsellor needs to avoid self projection just as much here as in all aspects of the counselling relationship. It is often helpful to ask key questions such as, 'How did you feel as you left the cage?' or 'How did you feel when you returned to the cage?' and a particularly useful question, 'Does the imagery reflect any aspect of your life at the present time?', which asks clients to take risks with disclosures, so this should not be posed in a probing or insistent manner.

One of the authors used this theme in an unusual context.

I was walking in the grounds at work, when I came across a colleague who appeared to be in a somewhat emotional state, confused, tense and frustrated. I was so impacted by this that I summoned up the courage to ask if he was OK, because he didn't look it. The colleague confirmed my perception when I commented on it. I took myself by surprise when I spontaneously asked him to close his eyes and imagine that he was a bird in a cage. He said he could do this and I talked him through an abridged version of the script. We didn't even discuss the experience afterwards, but he outwardly seemed to be much more relaxed and we went our separate ways. Some years later, he went on to train as an alternative healer and resigned his academic post to follow this as a full-time career. He later ascribed the impetus for this life change to the awareness that came as a result of the imagery created during the fantasy. He had found it to be a profound experience, which crystallised his dilemma and revealed to him changes he needed to make in his life if he was ever to be happy.

We are our own best experts. This notion attributed to Rogers implies that we already possess answers to our life dilemmas but they may not be available to us simply via rational thought, as in the example just recounted. Imagery generated from scripts can provide visual metaphors which clarify and play out these dilemmas in a way which offers clients access to meaning-making and decision-taking. It could be argued that using scripted imagery in this way is an intrinsically manipulative process. This is of course a possibility, which is why the scripts themselves must as far as possible be neutral and non-evaluative as well as washed free of author bias. Clients need to be provided with opportunities to make sense of their experience with the counsellor's support, not their solutions. The following examples demonstrate how clients can respond to the imagery in any way that they wish in order to develop their own solutions or reach their own conclusions.

Script: The wise person

The following theme, variations of which appear in several sources, used to be called 'The Wise Man' but in avoiding the obvious gender bias, is now called the 'The Wise Person'. When taking an individual or a group through this script, at least one of us has slipped into using the word 'man' instead of 'person' and care needs to be taken to avoid this mistake. After the usual suggestions for relaxation begin,

> I would like you to imagine that you are in the foothills of a mountain. . . . Become aware that you are about to go on a journey up the mountain. . . . How do you feel about the prospect of making this journey? . . . What are you wearing? . . . Are you carrying anything? . . . As you set off, take a good look around you. . . . What is the scenery like? . . . What is the weather like? . . . Feel the temperature of the air on any exposed skin. . . . As you walk along, be aware of the changing scenery and the view. . . . Take a deep breath and take in the smells around you. . . . What is the surface like that you are walking on? Is it rough or smooth; is it steep or sloping? . . . As you walk along you realise that it will soon be evening and the light will start to fade. . . . You can see a moon beginning to appear on the horizon and this will provide enough light for you to see by. . . . As you walk along in the evening light you remember that you had been told of a remote valley in the mountain where a wise person lives in a cave. . . . Reach the path that leads to the remote valley and decide to visit the wise person. Now follow that path. . . . In the distance, notice the flickering flames of a fire and as you approach, you see the wise person sitting by the fire at the entrance to a cave. . . . Now approach the firelight. . . . It doesn't seem appropriate to speak, so sit by the fire, listening to the sound of the flames and taking in the appearance of the wise person. . . . The face and body. . . . The dress. . . . The age. . . . How do you feel about being in the presence of the wise person? . . . Now, in imagination, become the wise person and looking through their eyes, be aware of how you feel about the person who has come to visit you. . . . Now as the wise person, begin to give your visitor some advice on how to live their life in a more meaningful way. . . . [longer pause] Now become yourself again and be aware of how you feel about the advice you have just received. . . . Instinctively you realise that it is time to leave, but before you go, the wise person gives you a gift, which is just right for you now. . . . Take a good look at the gift, feel its texture and shape and be aware of how you feel about this gift. . . . Now begin your journey back down the mountain. . . . As you walk, take out your gift and take another look at it and perhaps begin to reflect on what you might do with it in the future. . . . Now start to breathe a little more deeply. . . . Allow the images to fade. . . . Bringing some feeling back into the fingers and toes and gently bring your attention back to the room.

The power of the fantasy experience can often produce a profoundly meditative state. Clients need to be allowed a space to continue reflecting on the experience internally. A useful bridge between the end of the imagery and talking about the experience is to ask the client to draw the gift or one of the other key elements. The drawing can then become a useful starting point for discussion and reflection.

It also can be productive to ask about the gender of the wise person, if it is not immediately mentioned by the client. The script provided is gender neutral, but from our experience it is common for both men and women to choose 'a wise man'. Some clients however will spontaneously choose a woman. Others, usually women, will conjure up an initial image of a man and then change it because out of a sense of political correctness they feel that they ought to ascribe wisdom to a woman. The stereotype image of a wise person seems deeply rooted, cuts across cultures and for many emerges as an old man with a long flowing beard, a Merlin-like figure drawn from ancient myths and legends.

Script: Changing vistas

The next script provides a means of encouraging clients to get in touch with their own expertise, and also includes some simple hypnotic techniques that encourage a deeper level of relaxation. It is an extended script which has four major thematic elements to it. After a short relaxation begin,

Imagine that you are by the seashore . . . It doesn't have to be a place you know . . . Take a good look around and have the sense that you are looking through your own eyes . . . Don't see yourself there, be there . . . What can you see? . . . What is the weather like? . . . What does the sea look like? . . . Is it still and calm? . . . Or is it stormy? . . . Take a look along the shore to the left . . . and then to the right . . . What is the weather like? . . . What is the temperature of the air? . . . Feel the air on any exposed skin . . . Take a deeper breath and take in the smell of the sea . . . You may be able to taste the sea air on your lips . . . Are you sitting, standing or lying down? . . . What sort of surface are you on? . . . How do you feel about being in this place at this time? . . . Now let these images go and allow the scene to change . . .

You are seated in a room that contains nothing but a desk and a chair . . . You are seated at the desk and there are two blank sheets of paper in front of you . . . Now begin writing your name, over and over again, until you have filled the two sheets of paper . . . [longer pause] Now let these images go and allow the scene to change.

Now you are an animal in a zoo . . . Take the first image of an animal that comes . . . What kind on animal are you? . . . What is your cage or enclosure like? . . . Don't see yourself in the imagery. Actually be there, looking through your own eyes . . . How do you feel about being in this cage or enclosure? . . . Do you have a keeper and if you do, how do you feel about your keeper? . . . How do you feel about the people who come to see you in the zoo? . . . In imagination, see if you can find a way of leaving the cage or enclosure . . . What happens and how do you feel about leaving? . . . How do any visitors react to you getting out? . . . How does your keeper react? . . . In imagination, just go anywhere you like and do anything you wish. Allow the imagery to take you wherever it wants . . . [longer pause] Now, in imagination, find your way back to your cage or enclosure . . . If you manage to return, be aware about how you feel about being back and how your keeper feels about your return . . . Now let these images fade and change the scene again.

You are back by the seashore . . . Once again, be aware of the scenery, of what you can hear, the temperature, the smell and the taste of the sea air . . . Now build up the expectation that, in a short time, someone important to you will come along the shore . . . Notice this person in the distance and as they approach engage them in a conversation . . . Notice that the conversation turns to important questions in your life right now and that they make helpful comments . . . [longer pause] . . . Now in imagination end the conversation and say goodbye . . . And when it is right for you, breathe a little more deeply, let the images fade and begin to come back to the room. But don't rush from the feeling of relaxation.

After a preliminary discussion, there are various elements of the script that can be identified and addressed in more depth. The section by the seashore is intended to be a relaxing process, but again it is important not to predict how the client will respond to these images as we have cautioned earlier. The second section with repetitive writing is intended to induce a mild hypnotic trance through monotony or boredom, so that the client will seize on the next section as a relief from the monotonous task. Again there may be aspects of this section that, serendipitously, may be important. For example, it is not uncommon for married women who have changed their surnames, to find that they revert to their maiden name – an indication perhaps that during the imagery sequence they have regressed to a child-like or adolescent state.

The third section is similar in its theme to 'The Bird in the Cage' script offered earlier, and may have similar outcomes. It may be helpful to enquire about the personality or characteristics of the animal that is chosen, for example, 'What are monkeys like for you?' and how they feel about having made this choice. The fourth section offers the possibility of accessing an inner wisdom or expertise which may not be available to the conscious mind. Clients may be surprised by the identity of the person who comes along. One of the authors found himself in conversation with a dark-haired, older woman who posed some important existential questions. He interpreted this as representing his less accessible feminine side, or anima, but as we have suggested earlier it would not be appropriate to impose this sort of interpretation on the client's experience but work solely with their interpretation of meaning.

Script: The river

In this next example, one of the classic guided imagery themes we describe in Chapter 3, the River was adapted as a script for a client who was unwilling to verbalise what was happening during an imagery journey. However, in the past he had found visualisation exercises particularly helpful in relation to helping him cope with serious bouts of depression. He was about to go on holiday which tended to bring on depressive episodes and he wanted a calming image to use while he was away.

> I want you to imagine you are at the source of a river; it can be real or imaginary . . . Start with the image of the source of the river and build up the sense that you are going to follow its course . . . Take time to look around at the scenery where the river begins its journey . . . Look into the water . . . Is it clear or murky? . . . Does it gush or trickle from the ground? . . . What can you smell and taste in the air? . . . Now, in imagination begin to follow this stream . . . Look at the banks of your stream . . . Can you see any wildlife around? . . . How deep is the water now? . . . What is the river bed like? . . . How fast is the water flowing? . . . In your imagination, become the water and be aware of how you feel . . . What is your life like as the water? . . . Now become the river bank and be aware of what it feels like to be the bank . . . How do you feel about the river that flows beside you? . . . Now, in your imagination speak to the river . . . Just say whatever comes into your mind . . . [longer pause]. Now become the river and reply to the bank; whatever comes . . . Go along with the flow of the river down to where it meets the sea . . . Be the river and experience the sensation of joining the sea. How does it feel? . . . [longer pause] Now become the sea and be aware of how it feels at the place where the river becomes one with you . . . Now begin to let the images fade, begin to breathe a little more deeply and bring your attention back to the room.

In spite of this client's reluctance to put his imagery into words, he felt able to conduct the dialogue privately in his head and volunteer information from the experience. For this reason, a scripted format proved ideal for him and allowed him to experience the powerful images, without the need for spontaneously verbalising the experience. After the scripted fantasy journey he reported,

> I found it very easy to enter into this visualisation. I had a real river in my mind which I have visited many times and of which I have vivid memories. I could visualise it clearly and I was surprised how quickly I could become absorbed by the river. It was so gentle at its source. As it continued I could see the importance of the river and how it sustained the wildlife and cattle. I watched as it gathered strength and depth but I wasn't afraid. At times it was turbulent and very strong and then suddenly it was calm. I felt its power but also its gentleness – a strange mixture. When it reached the sea, at first I was overwhelmed by the vastness and difference of the sea to my river and felt hesitant, but when you asked me to become the sea, I was able to welcome the river to join me and I saw that the river had the potential to start the cycle all over again. I found this imagery very powerful and could see that as I allow my feelings to flow I can create potential for change. As it was a river I am familiar with and have visited it at regular intervals throughout my life, I found it comforting and could let myself really get into the imagery.

When the client was on his holiday, he sent the counsellor a postcard on which he had drawn a smiley face and reported that the powerful imagery of the river joining the sea helped him face and manage his feelings while he was away from home.

Delayed reactions or sleeper effects of the scripts

We have found that a high proportion of clients report how the emotional impact of a scripted imagery journey reverberates in the weeks that follow the session. This is an indication that the experience has had a significant impact and that the imagery is continuing to prompt reflection and insight working to the client's advantage, well after the initial exposure to the script.

Here is an example of a client who had been taken through the 'Rucksack' script in the previous session and the client asked to return to the theme.

Client:	I've been thinking this week I would like to go back to the rucksack and have another look inside. I need to let go of some things.
Counsellor:	Let's begin with a relaxation. Pay attention to your breathing and feel your muscles relaxing. Now take yourself to the place you visited last week, where you left your rucksack. What can you see?
Client:	I'm walking along a path . . . it's like a green pasture on one side and there is a cliff edge on the other. I'm not too close and the walking is easy. I want to find my rucksack.
Counsellor:	Look around you . . . do you remember where you put it?
Client:	Yes, I'm walking over to it . . . It's heavy and I covered it in leaves I didn't want anyone else to find it [longer pause]. I'm pulling on it. Oh, it's moving. At last I've got it!
Counsellor:	Can you describe it to me?
Client:	It is blue and grey and tightly done up, it's very heavy and very full.
Counsellor:	Would you like to undo it and look inside?
Client:	I'm unclasping it. It has some very big boulders inside, they're all different shapes.
Counsellor:	What do you want to do now?
Client:	I'm going to take one out, this one here – it's difficult to get a hold of because it's very smooth, but I've got it now.
Counsellor:	Describe it to me as you are holding it.
Client:	It's very smooth and cold and oh so heavy . . . I feel angry now, I feel angry with this boulder. I want to chip away at it – I want to destroy it.
Counsellor:	How might you do that?
Client:	I need a chisel or something. I'm looking round I've got to find something to help me.
Counsellor:	Can you see anything that might help?
Client:	[silence] Yes, there is a spade here under a bush [breathing getting shallower]. I'm hitting it with the spade but it isn't working. The spade just bounces off. I can't even chip it. I've thrown the spade down and I'm looking round now. I feel frustrated.
Counsellor:	What does frustrated feel like?
Client:	Tight, angry, mad with the boulder.

Counsellor: What would you like to do now?
Client: I want to throw the boulder away.
Counsellor: How are you going to do that?
Client: I'm dragging it to the edge. It's very heavy. How I managed to carry the rucksack up the mountain I don't know. I'm still dragging it to the cliff. It's such hard work, the boulder is so smooth, I can't get a grip. I want to swear. . .
Counsellor: Go on then, say whatever you need to say.
Client: I've got it to the edge, it's over the edge and I'm watching it bounce on the cliff face as it tumbles down [shallow breathing]. Oh!! It's just shattered into several pieces and they are going off in different directions. I feel exhausted.
Counsellor: What does exhausted feel like?
Client: My arms are heavy, my shoulders ache. My back hurts.
Counsellor: Take a few moments to recover and think what you would like to do now. Where is the rucksack?
Client: I'm going back to the rucksack. I've had a look inside and there is a big space now. Although there are still more boulders in it, I can see a space and I feel relieved. I can't do anymore today, I'm exhausted. I've let go of something very big today.
Counsellor: Now secure the rucksack once more and put it away again.
Client: I've put it back under the same bush and covered it with leaves.
Counsellor: Take one last look around, notice where you're leaving it and know that it is safe there and you can return to collect it whenever you wish. When you feel ready, begin to let go of the images and gently come back to the room. You might want to wriggle your fingers and toes, and perhaps stretch a little.

During the debrief of the imagery journey, this client disclosed his tendency to stubbornly hold grudges and he felt that a significant block had moved for him. In a later session, he described how his feelings towards his mother had changed and his attitude was now much more positive when he thought about her and he ascribed this to the self-awareness which emerged from the imagery journey and the subsequent processing work with the counsellor.

Further applications of scripts

Scripted guided imagery can be used with a group as a part of group therapy and with training groups that are concerned with personal or professional development. Many trainers involved in personal growth or personal development activities use guided imagery scripts in their work. It seems reasonable to assume that if guided imagery can make a contribution to psychological and physical well-being, then it can also help a fully functioning individual gain further insight into their own psycho-social functioning. Volunteer group members take readily to the process of guided imagery as they have come to the workshop highly motivated to change and grow. Stevens (1971) provides a useful set of scripts for working with groups whether for therapy or personal development and also provides practice guidelines for working with the subsequent responses from the group.

Increasing numbers of students in schools have been exposed to this activity through personal, social and emotional education (Hall et al., 1990). It has been used with all age groups from pre-schoolers to 18-year-olds, with disaffected students and young offenders. Some of the outcomes reported in our research of using imagery in schools include a more relaxed class, improved standards of creative writing, increased use of a feeling vocabulary to describe emotional responses, more powerfully evocative drawing, eagerness to participate in classroom discussion following the use of a script and high memorability. Often students request more imagery journeys and the technique has been used as a tool for more conventional forms of learning in the curriculum including science and maths. Our research has revealed no reports of negative outcomes from students arising out of these experiences. We have had a report from a teacher who used 'The Wise Person' script in a whole school assembly in a large comprehensive school. Again there were no negative outcomes reported from this activity and his colleagues reported that their classes seemed unusually relaxed for up to two hours after the assembly.

One particularly interesting educational application of guided imagery using scripts was in the teaching of human biology to trainee nurses (Gascoyne, 2005, personal communication). The teaching of human biology has always been problematic in nurse education because it is dealing with processes that are not directly observable and because these processes are described in words they are not immediately memorable. The assessment scores in human biology were consistently poor with a high proportion of students failing the tests. Gascoyne provided students with an imagery script to illuminate the biological processes involved in each of the lectures included in the module. The groups using imagery scripts achieved a dramatic improvement in the test scores for the human biology module. There was also evidence which showed that students were using their understanding of physiology more effectively in clinical practice.

In this chapter we have discussed a form of guided imagery which uses scripts which are read aloud to the client or groups. There is a growing practice literature of scripts designed for use in schools, educational contexts such as management development, personal coaching and for personal growth. One particularly useful source of scripts for counselling and psychotherapy is provided by Ferrucci (1982). Naparstek (1995) and Brigham (1994) provide scripts for healing using imagery and Naparstek's work is available commercially on CD and audiotape. She has designed scripts specifically for use with grief and loss, depression and general wellness. In the next chapter we go on to examine how drawing can be used to augment the benefits that can be gained from the use of guided imagery and further enhance opportunities for insight and learning.

6

Using Drawing to Explore Imagery

Colleague: I first 'drew my tree' when I was training to be a teacher. I was a bit sceptical but intrigued when Eric suggested it, and decided to have a go. My tree was a personal revelation and I can still see it as vividly today as the day I drew it, 30 years ago. Until that moment, I had never been able to acknowledge the vitality and enthusiasm for life, that I saw staring out at me from my branches and foliage. My poor self-image meant that I had never been able to admit a strength of purpose and commitment which were etched in every line of the trunk and root systems. For the first time in my life, I felt a vague sense of pride in myself. I have never forgotten that feeling and my work subsequently with students has been to help them find a way of tapping into their own inner potential, in the way I had been helped to do on that day.

One of the challenges facing counsellors using imagery as a therapeutic tool is that it is the client's private internal experience which is visually inaccessible to them other than by means of a verbal description. The counsellor will probably experience parallel images which are prompted either by the client's verbalisation or their own imagination, but we can be certain that the counsellor's imagery will be different from that of the client. However, images can be drawn as well as described in words and also modelled in clay, represented through photo montages, collages, music, dance and so on. The physical limitations of most counselling rooms make drawing the most likely option. In this chapter we focus on the reproduction and communication of images through the medium of drawing and how this artefact can be used to extend the client's understanding of their internal world. Readers will recognise elements of Art Therapy in this approach, but Art Therapy as discussed by Rubin (2001) is a much more fleshed out therapeutic system in its own right, although there is a discernable overlap with the approach we suggest here.

Clients can either be encouraged to draw to stimulate imagery or as a vehicle through which to discuss an earlier imagery experience. As a stimulus, the drawing is in front of the client and it is possible for them to engage in a guided imagery sequence without closing their eyes. Psychosynthesis offers an approach which is described as 'free drawing' in which the client is given drawing materials and invited to draw without even offering a specific theme. Ferrucci (1982) argues that drawing can access the unconscious and illuminate material that is not immediately accessible to our awareness. He suggests that drawing can provide a form of psychological catharsis or cleansing and provide a better understanding of our ongoing psychological processes. Clients may not expect drawing to be part of the counselling process and may be surprised at any suggestion to do this, in the same way that they may be startled by the suggestion to use guided imagery. Therefore the suggestion to use drawing has to be approached sensitively in order to avoid the client having the sense that the activity is in any way being imposed on them.

'But I can't draw!' This is a common cry from adults, including trainee counsellors, and it is probably related to their experiences of being 'taught' to draw in school. On the other hand, some clients relish the opportunity to draw, and enjoy representing their innermost thoughts and feelings through drawing as opposed to talking. At the other extreme there are clients who are terrified at attempting to doodle on paper. It is as if they feel that they might disclose something inadvertently about themselves which they would rather keep hidden or not acknowledge.

Drawing may conjure up connotations of representational, naturalistic sketches, whereas what we mean here is any attempt to depict an aspect of the imaginal experience in a graphic form. One of the authors regularly chooses broad swathes of colour; another prefers naturalistic drawing, while a third prefers to use a naïve or 'primitive' approach, such as stick drawings when responding to portraying imagery through drawing. What is clear is that the drawing here is primarily an act of self-expression and technique is unimportant. A parallel would be to use free writing or a stream of consciousness in writing as opposed to being asked to compose a sonnet.

Therapists need to discover their client's attitude to expressing themselves through drawing, stressing that this has nothing whatever to do with artistic or technical competence and that anything they draw is useful. If the client makes it clear that they are reluctant or anxious to draw, then this should be respected, but the feelings of anxiety might be worth discussing in a non-judgemental way, as it could represent a way in which the client limits their self-expression more generally.

Counsellor: What feelings does my suggestion that you do a drawing bring up for you?

And later:

Counsellor: Where do you think those feelings might have come from?
Counsellor: Is there any other way you might prefer/want to represent your experience of the fantasy/imagery?

The client may go on to try some squiggles with a biro on paper, which could be a lead in to producing a more substantial drawing with crayons, felt tips or pastels. It can be helpful if the counsellor also does a drawing at the same time and if it is the case, disclose any feelings about artistic limitations. Clients with perfectionist tendencies have difficulties with just 'messing about' with drawing and use their perceived lack of ability as an excuse for not taking part in the exercise. Paradoxically, just 'messing about' could well be an important developmental activity for them.

To introduce drawing into your work, it is helpful to have a collection of drawing materials available in or near to the counselling room. Pastels, charcoal, felt tip pens and wax crayons are all basic resources, but we have also known colleagues use materials such as pebbles, textiles, postcards along with scissors and glue to create montages. It is also helpful to have a range of sizes of paper at hand. Some clients prefer to have a large sheet of A2 paper which they cover with drawing, whereas others will choose a small piece of paper and then do a tiny drawing in one corner. The client can be asked about these choices:

Counsellor: What is happening in this blank space?

Or having taken on the role of an aspect or element of the drawing:

Counsellor: What does it feel like not to fit into the piece of paper?

Responses to these simple questions can lead to profound insights for the client and the act of breaking a habit, even with such an apparently simple task as using a crayon on paper, can prove to be an emotional experience and a model for further behaviour change outside the therapy room. Children and adolescents are, with a small number of exceptions, usually happy to do drawings. It is a particularly useful method when the young person or even some adult clients feel they lack verbal fluency or for whom English is not their first language. Some clients wish to keep their drawings and report displaying them on notice boards, walls or fridges at home and work. This reflects the emotional impact of the creative act itself and provides a reminder of the insights which were revealed. We have known clients who keep a series of drawings. They may refer back to these in relation to current issues, with comments such as:

Client: Oh! That's just like the way I felt when the lock on the gate in the wall was stuck and I couldn't open it.

The use of drawing to process guided imagery

The experience of guided imagery or scripted imagery is invariably powerful in its own right. However the experience often includes an image, which stands out for the client and is uniquely important to them. Inviting the client to draw this focal image does appear to add an additional dimension and deepen understanding of the image as well as amplifying the emotional impact of the experience. If the client enjoys drawing and feels comfortable with expressing themselves in this way, it can prove particularly rewarding. Volcanoes, rosebushes, gifts from wise persons and in particular, the abstract images that we discuss in Chapter 7 can provide potent stimuli for drawing and subsequent dialogue. An alternative is to suggest a free choice:

Counsellor: What image stands out for you from that experience? Try drawing or representing it on paper using colours and textures that feel right for you.

This means that the client decides which are the important images rather than the counsellor and has greater control over the process. The counsellor may be surprised by the client's choice but this open invitation is much closer to the person-centred approach which we advocate and encourage as far as possible. Following the imagery journey, a client usually remains in a calm, relaxed state for some while. The act of drawing provides a psychological bridge between the intensely private inner experience of the fantasy and the discussion through conversation. In the deeply reflective space, the client can begin to make some sense and meaning out of their experience in a detached but highly involved manner which is characteristic of what Zohar and Marshall (2000) call using their spiritual intelligence. Figure 6.1 provides an example of a drawing following a Volcano imagery journey.

Using drawing to express feelings and abstract ideas

The client will often spontaneously volunteer information about how they feel and counsellors should encourage this. Sometimes the expression of those feelings may be out of kilter or incongruent with the content, such as the client who describes his or her anger in a dull, flat monotone or describes the state of bliss looking bored. However, given the suggestion:

Counsellor: Try drawing the feeling, rather than talking about it.

Or:

Counsellor: Draw how it feels inside when you experience the anger.

clients will often welcome the opportunity and produce a drawing that has much more authority and veracity than when talking about the feeling. As a 9-year-old student once said, 'Pictures say more than words'.

Figure 6.1   Journey up a volcano

Drawing feelings can capture extremes which clients may not dare to express authentically during verbal exchanges. The client can then be invited to express the feeling more congruently using the drawing as a stimulus. A useful sequence to follow is:

- comment neutrally on the incongruence between the feeling and the expression of feeling
- invite the client to draw the feeling
- ask the client to describe the feeling aloud after the drawing has been completed
- rehearse a more congruent verbal expression of feeling
- set goals for practice outside the counselling room.

Figure 6.2   Representation of feelings

Most of us have at some time been punished for expressing strong feelings and may feel inhibited as a result. However this prohibition is usually absent from drawing. Anger, sadness, fear, love, jealousy, anxiety, happiness, guilt, shame and the whole range of human emotions can all be felt, expressed and analysed safely through drawings (see Figure 6. 2).

Clients will also talk about more abstract notions or feelings such as emptiness, constriction or heaviness. Converting such sensations into drawings reveal that these ideas are much more tangible than may at first have appeared to the counsellor or even to the client and drawing can reveal meaning underlying these sensations. We discuss ways to work with abstract images in Chapter 7 in more detail and suggest that any abstract idea introduced by the client can be used as a stimulus for spontaneous guided imagery or a drawing. Sensations in the body such as a tight throat,

Figure 6.3   Crossing out negative thoughts

a bursting head, a sinking feeling in the stomach or sad eyes can all be converted into drawings and sometimes simply the act of drawing can alleviate the impact of the feeling. Figure 6.3 represents the act of crossing out negative thoughts.

> *Client*: It's strange, but now I've talked about the drawing of the sinking feeling it seems to have vanished.

Using drawing to stimulate guided imagery

It is possible to begin a session with a drawing as a stimulus which is then developed into a guided imagery dialogue. In our experience, a theme which has particular impact is that of the drawing of a tree. Trees are deeply potent, even magical symbols for human beings. They nourish us at both literal and metaphoric levels and are ubiquitous images in children's and adult literature. The universality of the tree as part of the cultural, economic and emotional landscape of our lives makes it a potent stimulus for drawing.

The counsellor might give the simple instruction:

Counsellor: I want you to draw a tree. It doesn't have to be a tree you have seen; just draw your tree.

This permits the client to unconsciously project aspects of themselves into the drawing and provides rich material for reflection and dialogue. The tree as an natural object can be readily identified with, having an upright stance and branches that extend like arms and roots which are out of sight of external scrutiny. We have no experience of working with people from countries without trees and who may therefore not be able to relate to the image of a tree. However, one of the authors worked with a group of Icelandic school counsellors, who live in a limited treescape, and in response to this exercise, they produced a very dramatic set of tree drawings.

An interesting example drawn from counselling practice was of the client who was cynical about both counselling itself and the use of drawing. On being asked to draw a tree, he quickly drew two lines for the trunk and a wiggly line to represent the foliage. The whole process took about five seconds and having completed the drawing, put down the pen with a challenging look as if to say, 'Make something out of that!' The following dialogue ensued:

Counsellor: What's inside the middle of your trunk? [pointing to the centre of the drawing.]
Client: There's nothing there.
Counsellor: What's it like to have nothing inside?

The tree was then left to one side by mutual agreement and the subsequent session turned into a highly productive dialogue, which prompted a breakthrough in the relationship as the client's trust grew and the cynical façade fell away.

We would recommend using 'the tree' exercise with clients who wish to extend their self-knowledge and self-awareness.

Counsellor: I would like you to make a drawing of a tree. Use the paper and the crayons and felt tip pens in any way you wish. It doesn't have to be a tree you know. Draw your tree and just let me know when you feel you have finished.

When the client has completed the drawing:

Counsellor: OK. What I would like you to do is to focus on the drawing of the tree. You don't need to look at me while we are talking. Keep your attention on your tree. Now, in imagination see if you can become the tree. Don't see yourself as the tree; actually become the tree. Perhaps describe out loud what your life is like as the tree, as fully as you can.

From this point, the client can be guided using the dialogic techniques outlined in Chapter 2 – encouraging the use of the first person, and asking the client to become parts of the tree as they seem significant and perhaps even setting up conversations between the various parts of the tree, for example, roots and branches and so on. In our experience, trees produced by clients can be startlingly vivid representations of how we have experienced them as people in the counselling room. Shy, inexpressive clients often draw faint, shrinking trees with few leaves. A particularly dramatic tree drawing from a client involved a single tree on the edge of an escarpment that was being blown horizontal by a strong wind. Some trees will be luxuriant and covered in fruit and have animals living in them. Others will be completely bare with broken branches. There will be thick, strong trunks and fragile slender ones and just about every variety of tree imaginable. Some trees will be realistic and even be trees that the client is familiar with and others will be imaginative creations that may not even look like a tree to the eyes of the counsellor. Clients have even been know to use the paper to make a three-dimensional model of a tree. Upright branches or large knots or wounds in the trunk may superficially seem to represent male or female genitalia. Simplistic interpretations, however, should be resisted by the counsellor and rather ask non-directive question such as, 'What happened here?'.

Clients have little difficulty in anthropomorphising the experience of being a tree, though a small number of clients, especially those who have a botanical background are only comfortable working within the biological structures of a real tree. Some clients have been known to start out in this manner and then suddenly switch to a more imaginative engagement with the tree image. Aspects of the tree may not be visible to the eye from the drawing and it might be helpful to draw attention to these. For example, discussing the trunk, questions can be asked about what it is like inside the trunk and how the *inside* of the trunk feels about the bark on the outside. There may be movements of energy or sap rising in the trunk or roots of the tree. The roots of the tree may not be visible, but it is a reasonable assumption that there will be roots and the client can be asked: 'What are your roots like?'.

An exploration of the roots and their relationship to other parts of the tree can produce interesting insights. Or conversely the client might be asked: 'If your roots were visible, what would they look like?'.

In the absence of any outstanding features, for example, branches or leaves, there are usually three main characteristics to explore: the trunk, the branches, including any foliage or fruit and the root system. These can be explored as independent entities before asking the client to focus on the interrelationship of parts to the whole.

Counsellor.   How do you feel about your life as the tree right now?

This question provides an integrating effect, following an atomistic examination of parts of the self as represented by the tree. The following

Figure 6.4   Draw a tree

example is a particularly moving and poetic account by a client who wrote about her drawing of a tree (see Figure 6.4).

Client: I am a birch tree. Halfway up a mountainside I am growing, old, strong and gnarled with age. My trunk is sturdy and carries a scar from where an immense branch fell off. The limb broke away gradually and painfully as it tore my bark on the way down. When it had fallen, it lay at the foot of my trunk and disintegrated, piece by piece, rotting over the years, until nothing remained except a few shreds and furls of bark.

My roots are wide and well-balanced beneath me, spreading out in all directions to support me and hold me in this precarious place on the edge of the hill. Some of my roots grow over boulders. These rocks are cold and hard and pointed in places, but over time, my roots have grown used to them and moulded to their contours as they have crept over them and down into the earth. The thin mountain soil has been eroded from where my roots climb over the rocks but these places of exposure are where I can feel the warmth of the sun most on my roots. Elsewhere, the soil my roots sink deep into is rich, full of moisture from the ancient peat, providing me with the sustenance I need to support my branches which spread wide into the sky.

My branches are many and stem from a womb-like place at the top of my trunk; a curving nest I grow outwards from. My branches are strong and wide at the base, growing more fragile and delicate as they extend into twigs. My branches have long been moulded by the winds and wild weather of the mountain which batter my body each winter. So, my branches have learned to grow along and out rather than rising directly to the sky.

My leaves are beautiful, green and exquisite in the spring fading to yellow, like gold, and finally falling as a carpet in the autumn.

My bark is easily torn and marked, paper thin in places, but it is indestructible amongst trees. My wood rots quickly, but the bark remains and rolls into the most beautiful of sculptures; like ancient scrolls.

I grow as one of a group of birches in a ravine in the hillside, but I am set apart on my rocks, proud of my survival, like an old wise woman of the tribes.

The client went on to reflect on her story, providing her own compelling interpretation of the experience.

Client: I have long had an affinity with birch trees and at some of the most painful times in my life, or when I have had to make difficult decisions, I have chosen to sit beneath a birch. To me, they are hugely feminine trees, apparently delicate, but immensely strong. So, imagining myself as a tree was not difficult, but it did give me a clearer picture of my situation.

I felt like I was the tree. I felt the pain of losing one of my branches, like losing a part of myself. I think that this represents the abuse I have suffered in my life. Coming to terms with it, sifting through the pain has been like watching a branch gradually rot at my side. In order for me to fully heal, the branch couldn't just roll off down the hillside and magically disappear. It had to be faced and dealt with in all its broken horror, piece by piece, as I have dealt with the abuse, bit by bit, through counselling.

I couldn't imagine being a tree without a scar at my side. It is not a scar on the front of the trunk, but at the side, because the scar is not the sum total of who I am but it is part of me. One of the hardest lessons I have learned is that I cannot change the past and go through life pretending it isn't there. It will always be there, but I can choose how I live with that and learn methods of coping with it, acknowledging its influence on how I see the world and other people. This has made me stronger and more in control of my life and the decisions I make, just as the tree had become strong and well balanced.

The scar today looks like a scar that has not healed easily. It is not a neat straightforward line but a bumpy, lumpy scar that tells its own difficult history; a scar that has been opened and re-opened and so healed awkwardly over the years. The scar always has the potential to be re-opened again, as there are constant reminders of abuse in the media and through relationships with others, but each time it never re-opens to the depth it opened before, and so each opening in its turn contributes to the healing process.

I thought it was interesting that my tree was growing on the edge. I am attracted to the excitement of things on the edge and much of my emotional life has felt like it has been lived on the edge. The abuse I suffered as a child took away safe boundaries so I learnt to form my own, sometimes not very safe ones, and sometimes none at all. My roots growing over the rocks, learning to cope with their cold hardness represents to me the journey I have made to come to terms with the uncomfortable and dark aspects of my past. I have learned to encompass those aspects and expose them to the light; a daring to be vulnerable and so to enjoy the warmth of the sun on those newly naked parts.

I have often been ill during the winter months and, likewise, my tree has learned to survive and to adjust its growing behaviour in order to cope and to live through the onslaught of the harsh winter winds and wild weather.

I was afraid to acknowledge that I was a tree set apart from the others on the hillside, that I was different as I felt there was pride in this. But, I am proud of who I am and of my survival on the edge. Sometimes I have felt like I was toppling over and down the mountain but each time through the help of counselling I have managed to sink my roots down deeper into the earth in order to become better balanced and safer, more securely rooted on my hillside.

My tree imaginings also helped me to see becoming old as a woman in a more positive light as I have always been terrified of the thought of growing old, maybe as part of the regret of the lost years the abuse has taken away from me. Now, I feel happier to celebrate my womanhood from the place I find myself in.

Sequences of drawings

A portfolio of drawings collected from a series of guided imagery sessions can provide a client with a visual diary of their experience. This visual record serves a similar purpose to a learning journal. It provides material for the client to chart their progress and as in the previous example offer valuable clues as to what they still need to achieve. Clients can be encouraged to group drawings together and name them, for example, 'This is my Blue Period' or, 'These are my dark days'. The following abridged example provides an account of how a client made use of a series of drawings over a period of months and gives an indication of the significance to her of drawing in the development of her therapy.

Client: I started having counselling following a number of stressful events in my life – bereavement and the dependence of my surviving parent, workplace pressures. The counselling had been suggested by a good friend during a period that brought two sessions of absence from my employment. At first I was reluctant – I was not a 'head case' but eventually to 'shut her up' I decided to do it. I was fortunate to be given a list of Christian counsellors by my local vicar and after some further pondering I called. As a person I would not describe myself as a control freak but I do like order and I like to be in control. Socially, my self-esteem was virtually non-existent, thinking I was just tolerated by anyone I was with; this brought the consequence that I had opted out with my life revolving around work.

In the beginning I made the decision that I would go along with an open mind and was prepared to 'go with the flow' of what I was asked to think about/do. Quite early on she mentioned that people often like to draw what they were feeling. Not being very artistic I did not think that I would go down that route; however, on one occasion I was talking about how I felt when people kept asking me to do things that I found weighing me down. I was asked where these feelings went and I replied that it was like they were just pouring into the area at the base of my throat and choking me. It was suggested that I draw what it was like. As it was such a simple thing I did as she suggested, drawing something akin to a cone partially filled but continuing to fill up with lines of other things pouring into it. It is probably significant that I chose to use black out of all the colours that I was given to use. In a strange way it was actually comforting to look at the very simple picture and say yes that's what it felt like.

A few weeks later we were talking through how I felt in relation to others and the fact that I had built up a barrier between myself and others. I talked of having a net over me, a sort of exclusion zone, to stop people from getting close to me. It was suggested I might like to draw it. What emerged was a picture of a large net, chained so it couldn't be taken away and with ropes tying it down. It was represented by a box, with skull and crossbones above it and I was surrounded by question marks. The colours were bright. It would have been easy to take it at face value but I was asked questions to get me to explain what I had drawn; these questions made me think more deeply and often resulted in more things being added to the drawing.

'What were the question marks?' – these represented my thoughts and feelings. 'Where did the thoughts and feelings go?' – some were stopped by the net; others were allowed to be shown to the outside world: I added lines going from the question marks up to the net. 'What about what others said to me?' – the net stopped a lot but some fell like rain: I added black dots falling down. 'What happened to the dots?' – they joined all the stuff that poured into me in my previous picture of the cone and became a great black mass that covered the box and question marks and then poured down into my chest, shown like a black bag below the mass (I had to add a second piece of paper). There was a pipe that they channelled down into the bag and another that brought things back up to the surface. There was a plunger on the surface that kept the flow going down.

'Where was the real me?' I added a small yellow circle at the bottom of the bag which was covered by a black grid and the rest of the bag was scribbled in black. 'And where is God?' This was an issue for me – I drew flames to the side of the picture with a path leading to a black mass at the surface and a spade trying to dig through the grot.

The questions were an important part of getting me to explore how I felt, to help me to understand my situation. On this occasion, the drawing made me feel quite sad for the person that was stuck at the bottom of the bag. I knew it was me, yet at the same time it was as if it was someone else. It enabled me to view my situation as an outsider.

In the following weeks, we talked more about the defence that I had built up and I drew a further series of drawings. My drawings were not artistic in any way – they were very child-like with stick people. The fact that they were basic didn't matter. As each one was drawn, I began to understand myself better. And between each session I would ponder what was drawn and occasionally in the following week I would want to change it in some way or even draw another that was more accurate. This was illustrated by the drawings I did as I thought more about the defence/shell that existed between me and those around me. I drew a series of three pictures. In the first I was encased by a net that was kept away from me by rigid supports going out from my neck. I consistently used red and black when drawing me and whatever was immediately around me. This was reflecting how I felt inside. There wasn't much joy around at that time.

I was asked where everyone else was. I added four or five brightly coloured smiley people. I never put a smile on me. She asked me again where God was. He felt a long way away so I drew a small 'sun' in a corner as far away from me as I could.

I thought about this drawing as we talked more about me feeling like I had made a shell around me to protect me. This made me want to alter my image so the next drawing was me with a complete shell – maybe like an eggshell but stronger around my stick-like outline – keeping everyone from getting near me and hurting me. We went on to talk about where I felt safe and what my safe place would be. I started by imagining it a bit like an igloo. I was asked to draw it. My igloo didn't have a door of any sort and I was curled up inside.

I was asked if it was dark or light. It definitely wasn't dark but it wasn't daylight either – an orangey yellowy colour – I coloured the space around me.

I was asked what was it made of and what it felt like if I touched it. It was solid but not hard, quite soft but definitely tough and impenetrable – nothing could get in.

I was asked what colour it was – not dark, not grey, perhaps dark, reddy colour.

I began to realise what I seemed to be describing. My safe place was like a womb. It was warm, comfortable and safe. I have no idea if these were subconscious memories but in my mind, and even now, I can still evoke the sensation of safety that I felt when I drew the picture.

As time progressed I began to feel less fearful of the reaction of those around me and we talked of how I was feeling – again the paper came out. This time I drew a large bell-shaped flower with me standing at the bottom. I could see and hear outside the flower but I was right at the bottom. For the first time I used brighter colours when I drew me. I even had the hint of a smile.

I moved house – something I had thought about but had put too many obstacles in the way. Even though my house was a safe place I was not totally happy there. My counsellor encouraged me to investigate the possibility of moving. A few weeks after I had moved, with chaos still around me, we were talking about how I felt in the new house. I felt much more content. My counsellor suggested another drawing. This time it was a typical child's drawing of a house with me standing in the front door, bright clothes, big smile and a huge smiling sun shining down over me. We came back to looking at me and the shell that I had put up around me and looking back at the progress that I had made. My counsellor said that we had made a few chinks of light in the shell. I responded that maybe it wasn't so much a shell as a sieve . . . but then thought that that had too many holes in so I changed it to a colander. My counsellor asked what sort of colander – metal, round with small circular holes.

I took that thought away with me and pondered on it quite a bit. Yes, it was definitely a colander that was covering me and I was totally surrounded by it. But there was light coming through the holes and maybe I was just beginning to put a finger out of a hole.

The following week we came back to the idea of a colander. I said what I had been thinking about and I decided I would draw it. A large metal dome with spaces in it. I had one finger completely out through a hole, another one just beginning to work itself out and an eye pressed against the colander looking out. There was a huge sun outside and light was falling on my fingers poking through, on my eye, and also flooding through the holes. It felt very happy and warm. Again my counsellor asked me to describe the picture. Then she suggested I should question the colander. This was something she had suggested I might like to do in other situations in the past – this was one thing I had never felt happy to do, it felt really silly. I still felt odd about doing it but I was persuaded to give it a go, to put my picture on the chair in front of me – it was suggested that I might go and sit on the colander chair to answer the questions but I was not happy doing that.

My first question to the colander was, 'Why do I need to have you over me?' And it replied, 'you think you need me but you don't.' This last statement really shocked me – I was amazed at the way the conversation with the colander had gone. I was the one keeping it there; it didn't think it was needed any more.

I had gone to a reunion the weekend before; I had been quite unsure about whether this would be a good idea. I was not confident that actually anyone would even want to see me. The idea that I didn't need the protection of the colander made me think about how I was received at the reunion and it was quite a revelation to realise that, 'nobody had been unenthusiastic to see me'. OK there had been people who I had not seen eye-to-eye with in the past and everyone had special friends they wanted to meet up with, but I wasn't unwelcome and there was nothing in their response to indicate they'd rather I wasn't there – that perhaps they actually liked me.

My counsellor thought I should try lifting the colander a bit to see if I could cope. I said I was going to cut a flap in it and crawl out but I could always get back in and shut it down again – the igloo effect. During the week that followed I realised that I hadn't cut a flap, I had lifted it up so that the rim was vertical. I had put it up and hadn't dropped it down again . . . I hadn't needed it. In fact, it wasn't there, in my mind I had put it in the garage waiting to go to the charity shop! I felt so different. It really did feel as if a covering had been taken away and I could see all around me unhindered.

The use of imagery has certainly impacted a huge amount on me over the two years I have been having counselling. But it was not just the drawing of the pictures but getting me to describe each one; the questioning was a vital part of the process – what's it like, is it light or dark, hard or soft, colour, etc.? The pondering of each image through the following week was also important. The conversation I had with my colander was perhaps the most amazing experience thus far and also the most liberating.

Notice the features common to both accounts. The rich vivid descriptions of experience; the emotional and psychological lyricism of the descriptions; the minutiae observed as if through a microscope, which give the accounts authenticity and poignancy. The clients' own commentary also demonstrate the extent to which this life observed becomes a life better understood and finally becomes a vehicle for personal change and growth.

The accounts also provide examples of the way clients were drawing important conclusions for themselves; owning these conclusions and making their own interpretations. The counsellor is simply supporting the process without attempting to take responsibility for their client's learning, and it is interesting how confident the client feels in coming to her own conclusions and making value judgments about the counsellor's interventions. This account demonstrates how she never felt under pressure to conform to her counsellor's suggestions.

Research and drawing

Most of the academic research into the potential meaning and interpretation that can be applied to spontaneous drawing comes from work with children. A number of tests have been designed to gain a better understanding of their internal world. These invariably involve the use of human figures and are intended to provide information about the children's understanding of themselves and the significant people in their lives. Such tests have failed to demonstrate acceptable levels of reliability and validity as diagnostic tools (Thomas and Jolley, 1998), but as Burkitt (2004) argues, this does not mean that the drawings do not have emotional significance for the subjects themselves and it is not possible for an external observer to draw reliable 'conclusions' from any particular drawing. Burkitt reports that there appear to be some consistencies, such as a tendency to use dark colours for people who are viewed negatively and larger figures for individuals who are regarded as socially important or authority figures, but there are too many exceptions to this to base firm interpretations on the drawings.

An indication that adolescents' drawings following a scripted imagery journey of the life of a tree through the seasons generated a significant increase in the expression of feeling in later writing was provided by Hall and Kirkland (1984). Following the imagery journey and the subsequent drawing exercise, students were asked to write about the experience beginning, 'I am the tree and I . . . ' and to write in the first person, present tense. The writing about the life of the trees were suffused with feeling, just as in the adult examples we provided earlier and appeared to reflect important aspects of the students' lives. Here is a typical example from that adolescent group (punctuation and syntax uncorrected):

> I am the tree and I have no leaves, people don't care about me. They just swing on my young branches and bend my trunk. I have no feelings. I just sit there as miserable as could be my roots are thin and nobody looks at me. I bear no fruit and I'm really thin and ugly. The place I'm in is Horrible no one to talk to just stuck in the school garden and the children I see are horrible to me. They never stop and look at me they just say horrible things. I wish I could walk and talk to everyone and then I be horrible to them I would. I shout and scream like they did to me. The wind just blows me side to side I'm to weak to stop it my branches are nearly breaking off. I wish I could be free.

A small minority of the tree accounts were expressed in positive terms, but the overall picture was one of an expression of sadness, hurt and anger. Young adolescents often disown such feelings because they associate them with emotional vulnerability. If, however, this group are projecting aspects of their own experience, it would suggest that many adolescents do feel emotionally raw. This exercise was repeated with a larger adolescent cohort, involving four teachers and their classes and four imagery themes (Hall and Greenwood, 1986). The teachers involved in the research reported shock at the outpouring of emotion from the writing and said that they now saw the students in a totally different light. They were also surprised by the improved quality of the students' writing, which emerged from the written accounts.

Teachers and counsellors may wish to debate whether the encouragement to express feeling is a good thing. Certainly, there is an explicit assumption in much of the literature in counselling and psychotherapy that the understanding and appropriate expression of feeling is a healing and growthful activity, although this has been questioned in some contexts (Ellis and Cromby, 2004). If this assumption is correct, then it is a reasonable extrapolation to assume that the experience was cathartic for those students and would be likely to lessen the distorted acting out of feeling that adolescents can indulge in. Hall et al. (1990) provide a description of ways of using imagery and drawing as part of the personal and social development curriculum for students of all ages in schools. This was done through the use of scripts working with whole classes or sub-groups of students. As part of our research, we collected a large sample of reports from teachers who tried out these approaches and received no reports of negative outcomes. Nor were there complaints from parents or students, who consistently requested additional imagery journeys.

This chapter has focused on drawing, though, as we indicated at the beginning, there are many other ways in which art forms can be used to provide an external expression of the experience of imagery and provide the counsellor with an indication of the client's inner world that goes beyond verbal description. Working with clay, for example, appears to involve strong, often primitive feelings. However, clay can be a 'messy' medium, involving preparation before the session and does not fit readily into a series of 50-minute sessions where the counsellor may have to move from one room to another. Paper crayons and felt tip pens are inexpensive and portable. In the next chapter we explore working with spontaneous and abstract images, which also provide further opportunities for drawing as an aid to self-awareness and personal growth.

7

Working with Spontaneously Generated Imagery

Our emotions are both preceded and accompanied by images. Our stress is created by perceptions and images. Our relationships are mightily affected by the images that accompany our core beliefs. The ways in which we relate to the world and to others are dictated by our images of ourselves and how we imagine our futures.

(Deirdre Davis Brigham, 1994: 33)

One of the most basic human drives is to make ourselves real, visible to others. Essentially to be understood. Clients enter therapy, whether they are aware of it or not, in the hope that in being more vividly seen by the counsellor they will become, as if by magic, more visible to themselves. Having temporarily lost, or forgotten, how to make sense of and piece together the jigsaw of their lives, they look to the counsellor to make patterns from the fragments they place before them. These fragments often come in the form of images, similes and metaphors.

Client: My life feels as if I am crawling through a sewer with no light at the end.
Client: I feel like I'm drowning in tears.
Client: My world has been reduced to a windowless room with walls closing in on me.

In this chapter we consider the ways in which these spontaneously occurring fragments of imagery, which emerge in the form of symbols, metaphors and similes can be used in the therapeutic encounter. Everyday language is peppered with imagery which may become more intense or vivid in the therapeutic dialogue when the individual is struggling to make sense of their own experience or to be more profoundly understood.

It is the therapist's task to tune in to the client's use of these images and work with them creatively to help restore meaning and feeling of integration or wholeness. However, such similes and metaphors do not necessarily stand out as clearly when they are more commonplace or less extended, because they are merely a natural part of our conversations. Statements like, 'I feel under pressure' are used so often, it becomes difficult not to hear them as literal statements. Listening for and identifying these images requires a high degree of concentration and focus on the part of the counsellor. With focused attention, however, they will begin to stand out like contours on the emotional map of the client's inner life and provide the counsellor with the potential for greater empathic awareness of the client's experience. The sensory modalities of the client should also be noted in order to heighten empathic understanding.

We suggest that spontaneously generated images, however fragmentary, are among the most potent sources of data for the counsellor about the psychological state of the client. They will have emerged directly from the client's inner world and best illustrate the important themes that are currently exercising them. Counsellors may use metaphors or similes to signal that they have empathic insight into the client's experience or state of mind:

Counsellor: It sounds like the events you describe have been like going through a nightmare for you.

Or:

Counsellor: The opportunity to share your grief seemed to be like an oasis in the middle of an emotional desert.

The examples we have provided so far are first of clients who spontaneously use imagery to convey the nature of their emotional experience and secondly, of counsellors using imagery to reflect back their perception of the emotional state to the client. Another approach is to ask the client to provide an image themselves which best encapsulates the events or relationships they seek to describe. This can be done indirectly:

Counsellor: What does it feel like to be in this relationship with no way of escaping?

This may or may not produce an image that would be useful to work with and whether it does or not, it is still a useful question to ask. Alternatively, the counsellor can directly ask for an image.

Counsellor: Can you think of an image that would for you, best sum up the situation you feel you are in right now?

Or:

Counsellor: Is there an image that you think might be helpful to you when you begin to get anxious?

The following example involves a client who was experiencing problems with her weight. She had tried all manner of diets without success. She wanted desperately to lose weight with a view to becoming pregnant. Her self-esteem was poor and she was clearly unhappy with her life.

Ironically, she enjoyed a very successful career and was highly regarded in her profession. She initially was resistant to any suggestions of using imagery techniques. For her, it didn't make sense. However after several counselling sessions and without much success in changing her eating habits, the following dialogue took place.

Client: This is going to sound really weird but I often hear a voice encouraging me to eat more when I don't want to. Like I might stand at the fridge and I'll be encouraged to eat things that are in there. I find it really hard to resist. It'll say to me, 'go on; no one will know and after all, don't you deserve it?'

Counsellor: What sort of image do you feel this voice has?

Client: I've never thought of that, it just seems to be there . . . [short pause] it's a monster, definitely a monster.

Counsellor: What would you like to happen?

Client: I want it to leave me alone. I've never told anyone this, it's really crazy.

Counsellor: I'd like you to imagine your monster and describe it to me.

Client: Oh, it's enormous with big eyes, a big mouth . . . it's ugly. I don't want to talk about it.

Counsellor: I'm going to ask you to talk to this monster and begin a conversation with it. Do you feel able to do that?

Client: I'm not sure, it seems very strange. Over the years I've tried so hard to ignore it. I know I can't talk out loud but I'll try to talk in my head.

Counsellor: That's a good start. Just begin by telling it what you feel and think of it and what you would like to happen. . . . [long pause]

Client: I've told it to leave me alone, that I know what food is good for me and when I need to eat. I've told it that . . . I can manage without it now and that I'm not going to take any more notice of it.

Counsellor: What is happening to the monster while you talk to it?

Client: Well, the strangest thing is happening – I am getting much bigger, I think I must have been quite small with this monster and now as I watch I am getting much bigger than it.

Counsellor: What would you like to do with the monster now?

Client: I'm going to put it in my old school trunk – I've done that and now I'm sitting on the trunk.

Counsellor: What else is happening?

Client: I can hear it scratching to get out, but as I sit here it's getting fainter and fainter and I feel stronger . . . [long pause] I feel as if I have control now – not the monster.

After this session the client made significant progress in changing her eating habits and began a programme of exercise. Over the months she began to lose weight and felt she had more control over what and when she ate. She also became pregnant and managed to retain control of her eating habits during the pregnancy. With hindsight it was possible to see that this session was the pivotal moment when she took an important step forward, taking the risk to let the imagery reveal to her conscious mind what she had previously hidden.

The following example is also a client's first exposure to working with spontaneously generated imagery and was part of a time-limited contract of seven sessions in a GP practice. She had been off work with stress and was faced with making important decisions in her life. During the first four sessions she explored with the counsellor her life situation, the options that were open to her and what was holding her back from realising her goals. When she arrived for the fifth session, she reported feelings of despondency, had no energy and felt her confidence had completely disappeared. She had also put on a great deal of weight while off work and talked about feeling trapped.

Client:	I feel so trapped, there are many decisions that I need to make but I just can't; I haven't the confidence and I feel trapped.
Counsellor:	What does being trapped feel like?
Client:	Being in a room with no doors, no windows – stuck!

The client was so completely absorbed by the image that it was judged appropriate to go straight into discussing it without the preparation of a preliminary relaxation exercise.

Counsellor:	Can you imagine yourself in that room?
Client:	Oh yes, I'm very familiar with it.
Counsellor:	Look around the room and describe it to me.
Client:	I'm standing in the middle; the walls are all very dark there is no furniture. There is a light in the middle of the ceiling but it doesn't reach the corners, I feel so depressed.
Counsellor:	I'd like you to stay with that image for just a little while. I know it's not very comfortable for you but please try. I'd like you to walk round the edges of the room to explore the dark corners where the light doesn't reach.
Client:	I'm not very happy doing that.
Counsellor:	Just take it very slowly. If it feels too much for you then we will stop at any time.
Client:	Well I'll try . . . I'm walking around one wall, which is solid. There is no way for me to escape. I feel so trapped.
Counsellor:	What does that feel like?
Client:	Stuck, exhausted, pointless, frustrating. . . . [long pause]
Counsellor:	Stay with those feelings, what would you like to do now?
Client:	I'm going to feel my way around the corners of the room [pause] I've found something! It seems like an old door which has been locked for ages. I've found the handle. Oh, [disappointment in voice] it's locked. Just a minute, there's a key. It's very rusty and it's very hard to turn. I don't think I shall be able to open the door. I feel like giving up. [she sounded very despondent.]
Counsellor:	What would you like to do now? . . . [short pause]
Client:	I'm going to try and open it . . . I'm turning the handle. It's stiff but it's moving . . . I've opened it. Oh!!! Wow!!! I'm looking through it and the view is so lovely. It's countryside, fields, hedges and the sun is shining.

Counsellor: Can you move through it?

Client: I've just seen a bench to the right of the door, I'm going to sit on that and look at the view. That's very strange; my cat is on the bench already. I'm now sitting on it stroking my cat. I want to stop now.

The client sat in silence for a while after this intervention. At the end of the session she decided to write down all her options for the future. The two subsequent sessions she talked about feeling more confident about the possibilities open to her. At the final session she talked about the steps she had taken towards returning to work. The breakthrough for this client was the moment of insight which came from working with the image of feeling trapped in a room with no doors.

Spontaneously generated images are particularly beneficial to clients on time-limited contracts which are imposed by agencies such as doctors' surgeries. Using thematic approaches to guided imagery will invariably take up a whole session and possibly part of the previous session as preparation. Using interventions that relate to the clients' spontaneous reports of their experience can get to the heart of issues more quickly and can be worked within a much shorter time frame. This will also depend to some extent on the expertise of the counsellor and the level of trust which exists in the therapeutic relationship.

The following example is from a client who had anxieties related to fear of failure in her job. She had a stressful managerial role and a very hectic home life. She found it difficult to relax and had a disturbed sleep pattern.

Client: My anxiety is overwhelming. I was up at 4.00 am again today. I can't relax.

Counsellor: That must be exhausting for you. Where do you experience the feeling of overwhelming anxiety?

Client: It is in my stomach and my head. It's like churning butterflies in my stomach but it's worse in my head. My head is full of anxiety.

Counsellor: Can you say what's in your head?

Client: Yes, loads of anxious thoughts. I am frantically thinking I should be able to cope. I ought to be responsible for more things. I should be able to make more decisions. I feel like I'm a failure.

This client is aware that her current thinking patterns are to some extent irrational. She has worked on challenging these but forgets to do it outside sessions and then blames herself for being inconsistent. This negative spiral needed to be interrupted if she was to make progress in her therapy.

Counsellor: Can you try to imagine your anxious, racing thoughts as an image in your head?

Client: Yes. It's sort of like ticker-tape always running, streaming past at great speed.

Counsellor: What do you need to make that tape slow down or stop?

Client:	Well, mmmm. It needs someone to switch off the machine.
Counsellor:	Have you an idea where the machine is located?
Client:	No. But it is definitely outside me and I have no control over it.

This client had expressed a strong need to be in total control of all aspects of her life.

Counsellor:	Could you try to imagine some kind of buffer between you and the streaming tape?
Client:	Yes, maybe a bucket to catch the tape.
Counsellor:	Would you like to try that?
Client:	Yes.
Counsellor:	OK. Can you breathe a little more deeply and maybe it would help if you closed your eyes.
Client:	Yes. The bucket is filling up very quickly.
Counsellor:	What do you want to do with the bucket when it's full?
Client:	I might need it.
Counsellor:	OK. Could you store the full bucket outside your head and perhaps bring in a empty bucket?
Client:	Yes, I'm doing that.
Counsellor:	How does that feel?
Client:	Good, but it is hard to do in my head.
Counsellor:	How can you soothe your head now? Can you think of a soothing image?
Client:	Yes, I can imagine clear, cool water being sprayed on my head, in my mind. That feels good.
Counsellor:	Good. Just relax for a while.
Client:	Yes, that is good.
Counsellor:	Ok, how is the tummy feeling now?
Client:	That's a bit better but I still have the churning butterflies there . . .
Counsellor:	What do you need to help with that?
Client:	I need something to flatten it.
Counsellor:	Can you imagine in your mind's eye that you are making the churning flatten?
Client:	Yes, that is good! [client sounded very surprised]
Counsellor:	Can you make it smaller?
Client:	Yes, I can.
Counsellor:	When it's really small you could perhaps breathe it out with the next few breaths or perhaps you would rather leave it inside you.
Client:	I can breathe it out. That's good. I feel much, much better.

The session ended with the client agreeing to use the images the next time she felt anxious at work, at home or during the night. She reported later that the imagery had proved beneficial and that her anxious thoughts were considerably reduced.

The following example is of a client who was sexually abused as a child by a family member and had endured a very public court case. Consequently the family's history was well known in her home town.

During counselling it emerged that she felt very vulnerable and exposed in social settings and imagined that everyone knew about and remembered her background of abuse.

Client:	I am very lonely because I don't know how to make friends or what to say to people. I feel as if they see right through me and know all about my background. At home I have had strangers come up to me and ask if I was 'X' and then talk about the court case. It's horrible, I feel so exposed. So now when I am out at the pub, I just sit quietly and don't know how to speak to the others. I'm avoiding going out.
Counsellor:	It sounds as if you need some protection for yourself and to feel in control of the personal information you give to others. Maybe we need to create something to help you feel separate and safe.
Client:	Yes, that sounds good.
Counsellor:	What image do you think would give you the feeling of protection when you are out with others at the pub?
Client:	A coat perhaps? No, I know, a raincoat.
Counsellor:	I want you now to imagine yourself standing in the hallway of your home, you are preparing to go out with a few friends for a drink at the pub and you are putting on a raincoat. Describe what you see.
Client:	I have a bright yellow raincoat and I'm putting it on. It's very long, stopping at my ankles and the sleeves are long as well. The buttons are very big, shiny black buttons and I'm doing it up to the neck.
Counsellor:	How does it feel wearing it?
Client:	It's very warm but not heavy and although it covers me completely, I don't feel restricted by it. I like it and it even has pockets for my hands so I'm totally covered.
Counsellor:	Now, begin to imagine you are in the pub with your friends.
Client:	We are sitting around the table and as usual I am at the end, feeling rather out of the group just watching. They are all laughing and talking and I want to join in but don't know how to.
Counsellor:	What have you done recently that you could talk about?
Client:	I've played badminton. Perhaps I could talk about that but I don't want them asking questions about my past.
Counsellor:	Look at your raincoat, is it still covering you?
Client:	Yes.
Counsellor:	Now in your imagination, see if you can become the raincoat. What might the raincoat have to say to you?
Client:	Oh I don't know . . . Let me think. Perhaps it wants to stop me getting wet.
Counsellor:	Go ahead then, I am the raincoat and I. . . .
Client:	I am the raincoat and I am covering you completely, you won't get wet when you wear me and no one can see what you are wearing underneath me. All they see is me, a beautiful yellow raincoat. . . .
Counsellor:	Now become yourself again, how does it feel to hear that?

Client: Good. Maybe I can take a small risk now, knowing the raincoat will protect me. I am now talking about badminton to the person next to me. She is interested . . . I feel quite wobbly but the raincoat is there.

Counsellor: How are the other people reacting to you?

Client: They are talking normally, no one sees the raincoat but I know it is there. Now someone is asking me something about my past . . . I feel very unsafe. [long pause]

Counsellor: What's happening now?

Client: I looked to the raincoat and put my hands in the pockets then just answered the question and do you know what? It felt OK. I only said what I wanted to say and no one knew any more. The raincoat has helped me.

Counsellor: Now imagine yourself returning home after the evening out and taking off the raincoat . . .

Client: I am in the hallway again and I have taken off the lovely yellow raincoat and hung it by the door. I feel complete. No one has taken little bits of me.

Counsellor: When you are ready, let go of the imagery and come back to the room.

In the ensuing discussion, the client agreed to practise emotional self-protection using the imagery at home and in social situations. She later reported gains in self-confidence and managed to talk comfortably about her background to friends without feeling she had exposed herself unduly. She later even went with a group of friends on a trip to Europe which she said she enjoyed immensely. The counsellor's ability to identify and work with a potent image had helped to provide a self-regulatory control mechanism for the client which was a breakthrough in her therapy.

In the next example, we give an account of an anxious client who suffered from both depression and anxiety and during a therapy session generated a spontaneous image from memory of herself as a young child hiding under a table.

She was encouraged to draw this image (see Figure 7.1; developed into Figure 7.2 in a later session). When the drawing was complete she began to disclose her old childhood fears and the impact of her past life experience on her present life. The anxious feeling was experienced as a sensation in the abdominal area. She was asked to imagine that she was very small and to go down inside her body to take a look at the problem. As a Christian she felt very worried about anything 'magical' and so she was encouraged to take an image of Jesus Christ with her in order to hold on to her belief. She chose a picture of Christ holding a light. Together they looked at the anxious tummy and she left Christ's lantern behind at the end of her journey. Afterwards, the client reported immediate relief from the anxiety and for several weeks continued to use the imagery sequence at home, ultimately helping her to reduce the symptoms of anxiety by having a simple coping strategy if the feelings began.

Figure 7.1   Spontaneous childhood memory

Figure 7.2   Spontaneous childhood memory: a later development

The following case provides an example of a client whose spontaneously generated image had a clear link with an earlier childhood experience. He had suffered with depression for many years. During one
session he began to explore his feelings and he mentioned that the
depression felt like a monster that overwhelmed him.

Counsellor:	If you were to face this monster, what would you need to protect you?
Client:	I think I'd need a shield that I could hide behind, a big shield that would cover me.
Counsellor:	Well, just begin to relax now. Become aware of your breathing and let the tension drop from your body. Now in your imagination, see yourself approaching the monster. You don't need to go too near and remember you have your shield to protect you. When you are ready, describe what you can see.
Client:	It's quite frightening and I'm holding the shield very tight, but I can see this monster. I don't want to get too close, but I'll try . . . It's very large and black and it's very tall. It has lots of heads which are all turned towards me and it wants to consume me. It wants to eat me.
Counsellor:	What do you want to do now?
Client:	I want to shout at it. I want to swear at it.
Counsellor:	Could you try to do that now?
Client:	Oh no! There are other people in the building and the people in the next room will hear me. I couldn't do that.
Counsellor:	Could you imagine yourself shouting at the monster?
Client:	Yes, I can give that a try. I'm standing and looking at it and it's trying to reach me, but I'm shouting and swearing at it. It really feels good.
Counsellor:	Is there anything else you can do?
Client:	Yes, there are some stones and I'm going to throw them at the monster.
Counsellor:	Describe what you are doing.
Client:	I'm hiding behind the shield and throwing the stones. They're hitting the monster and it's very surprised, as if no one has done that to it before. It's turning around and beginning to go away. Well, what a surprise. I never thought that would happen.
Counsellor:	What do you want to do now?
Client:	I'm going to leave my shield here to commemorate where I faced the monster and won.

During the discussion, the client also recalled a childhood incident at school. He had been bullied on several occasions, but on one particular occasion, he had managed to protect himself and the bullying had stopped. He felt he had reconnected with that sense of personal power which had lain dormant for a very long time. In a subsequent session, he reported that the visualisation had given him a sense of control over his situation and had helped him make some progress out of his depressed state.

Working with abstract images

Concrete images such as a shield, a raincoat, or a colander are objects that we recognise from everyday experience. Other images such as the wind, a movement of energy and even feelings themselves might also be available to awareness through the senses but related to kinaesthetic, auditory, olfactory and other senses than visual. These concepts can still be worked with in imagination by asking clients to provide visual images to represent them. Gerard (1964) supports the technique of encouraging clients to generate images for emotional states as part of the psychosynthesis tradition.

In Chapter 5 we gave the example of the client who drew his tree and described the trunk of his tree as having 'nothing inside'. 'Nothing' is an abstract notion and yet the client can be encouraged to transform the abstract into the concrete. 'Become the nothingness', is a prompt which the counsellor can use to initiate this process. Such abstract images are particularly potent and can represent important existential issues in the client's life. As with the spontaneously generated images described above, counsellors need to tune into these clues that the client may offer but which the clients themselves refuse to hear or engage with.

As we have seen, abstract images emerge from both the guided imagery journeys and the ongoing dialogue during a counselling session. In both categories they can be difficult to notice because they may be submerged in the flow of the client's talk. As you become more attuned to listening for them, they will begin to stand out like rocks in a stream and it is then possible to make an intuitive decision as to whether to interrupt the flow and engage with the image in more detail. 'Nothingness', 'hope', 'emptiness' are examples of abstract concepts which can be explored.

Here is a further example of working with the idea of 'nothingness' which is also linked to 'emptiness' raised by a female client who was a Christian, to describe her present life.

Client: I feel that my existence is nothing – empty.
Counsellor: Can you imagine this nothingness, emptiness, as any kind of image?
Client: It's a huge dark cloud, following me, enveloping and overwhelming me. I feel I'm helpless, lost, nothing.
Counsellor: Would you like to explore that in a little more depth?

After a long silence:

Client: Well in Gethsemane there was no relief, no escape for Christ. The father did not let him off the hook. He had to endure the aloneness and the separation from God. Maybe the reality is that the dark cloud is my Gethsemane, my path of suffering. Living in such darkness is so awful, I feel it's a sentence of lifetime nothingness.
Counsellor: You have told me that you believe that nothing can separate you from the love of God. Is there any way that you can see God in this dark cloud?
Client: Yes, I know that God must be there, but it's so hard.
Counsellor: Can you imagine an image which would help in those dark times? Is there a special place where you feel at peace?

Client:	Yes. In California, there is a wooded close, high up in the mountain overlooking the lake.
Counsellor:	Would you like to relax and imagine you're there in that special place? Close your eyes if you prefer and breathe a little more deeply. With every breath, you will be more relaxed. Now just imagine you are approaching the wooded close. What's that experience like for you?
Client:	It's warm. The sky is azure blue, the sun is shining down on the close. There are no clouds. It's very inviting. The birds are singing. I see the lake sparkling below.
Counsellor:	Is there somewhere you can sit?
Client:	Oh yes. There is beautiful soft green grass. I'm sitting on the grass looking up at the mountain now.
Counsellor:	How does that feel?
Client:	Wonderfully warm and peaceful. I'm so content here. The smell is fresh and there are fir cones on the grass.
Counsellor:	Stay in your special place for a while. Relax. Let the healing rays of the sun touch you. Let the warmth touch your body and your mind.
Client:	That's so good, I could stay for ever. I can feel the sun reaching me, embracing me.
Counsellor:	Can you hold this special place and these good feelings in your memory?
Client:	Yes, but I don't want to leave.
Counsellor:	You can revisit your special place whenever you feel that life is empty. Just relax and take the time to recall your special place from your memory. It will be there waiting for you. Just take one last look now and then come back into the room. There is no rush, just savour each moment.
Client:	I feel so refreshed and quite light inside.

This client is learning gradually to come to grips with strong feelings of nothingness and emptiness in her life. She has now begun to practise relaxation techniques, and uses the imagery of the special place regularly. As a result she reports that her stress levels have reduced considerably. She was also learning to put a value on herself by daring to do more enjoyable things outdoors. The connection she made between the suffering of Christ and her own dark cloud was undoubtedly spiritually meaningful for her and the exploration of the safe place imagery offered the promise of spiritual repose in an otherwise overwhelmingly bleak vision of the future.

This next client was also experiencing feelings of being overcome by her depression. She was also very frustrated and impatient with herself for not moving on as quickly as she would have wished in therapy.

Client:	I feel as if I'm in a black hole and I can't get out although I try hard.
Counsellor:	Can you become the black hole and try to get to know it better. You could say, 'I am the black hole and I . . .', followed by whatever comes into your mind.

Client:	OK. I am the black hole and I know you very well. I've been with you for ever.
Counsellor:	Ask it how long it has been with you.
Client:	How long have you been with me?
Client:	[replies to self] Since you were 13 or more.
Client:	Why are you here?
Client:	[replies to self] I have been stopping you from exploding for years.

The client had had a rigid upbringing and had experienced difficulty in coping during her adolescent years. She often felt angry and frustrated by the limits imposed upon her, which left her with the feeling of being shrouded in depression. During counselling, the client's depression had lifted, exposing huge unresolved feelings of frustration, resentment, fear of failure and anger. She said she often felt emotionally 14 to 15 years of age. The image of the 'black hole of depression' helped her to understand her feelings in a new way, bringing awareness and insight into a previously confused and frustrating area of her interpersonal relationships.

In the next example, a long-term client had a fear of exposure. Consequently he had developed the habit of triple checking every thought before speaking or taking any action. The long-term effect of this powerful defence mechanism had been increasing social isolation: an issue he raised during a counselling session.

Counsellor:	Can you find an image for this feeling of isolation?
Client:	It's like a dark figure shrouding me from the outside world. I hate it but it's seductive. It's so easy to stay in it. It's safe. I know it well.

By working with this image in subsequent sessions the client has learned much more about the way this dark figure acts as a defence and is daring to let it go very gradually and emerge from the safety of his isolation. He is actively using his own images as a measure of his therapeutic progress.

The spontaneously generated images, both concrete and abstract that have been reported in this chapter were unique to the clients involved. We hope that the reader finds them interesting and be intrigued enough by the reported therapeutic outcomes to try these types of interventions for themselves. The emotional impact of an image will be unique to the client and in all likelihood will not be shared by the counsellor. However, the empathic bond created by working with the client's spontaneously generated imagery will permit the counsellor an unexpected and privileged glimpse into the inner landscape of their world. Even when a counsellor does not share a belief system, for example, in the imagery involving Christian belief cited earlier, these are important generative metaphors for the client and need to be worked sensitively and respectfully.

By simply accepting and working with the images that the client generates, the counsellor is tuning in to the pre-verbal, 'forgotten language' described by Fromm (1951) which has not been distorted by the limitations of language and is making more effective psychological contact with both present and past experiences of the client's inner world. Once the counsellor is able to 'see' the client more clearly, they can then work together to put the jigsaw together and make sense of the whole picture.

8

Bringing the Body Alive

I Sing the Body Electric

(Walt Whitman, *Leaves of Grass*)

Therapists who use imagery in their work quickly begin to notice the connection between imagery and bodily sensation. Walking up a mountain path may produce sensations of tiredness in the legs. Floating in water may produce a feeling of relaxation. Confronting a monster prompts a drench of fear. A heightened sensation of a flow of energy becomes an electric current through the body. Asking the client to breathe a little more deeply can even exaggerate or heighten the sensations and feelings which are being experienced. It is these in the body experiences or sensations which provide the client with an extended range of data to understand and make sense of their experience. Traditional talking cures are constrained by the very language they rely on to produce self-awareness. Introducing imagery work into the therapeutic hour adds a further dimension by which to understand a client's world. Paying attention to the bodily experience generated by the imagery will then make the experience three-dimensional.

In this chapter we discuss a range of ways in which the use of guided imagery can be related to what is simultaneously happening in the body. We make the assumption that imagery provides a metaphorical awareness of the individual's 'being in the world' and that the body is reacting as if the episode recounted in the imagery journey is an authentic one. We are used to communicating meaning with words, but imagery and resulting bodily sensations appear to provide insights that would not necessarily emerge through verbalisation of experience alone and it may be that these different forms of experience are mediated through different pathways in the brain, as we discuss later.

Freud talked about women as the 'dark continent', but for many of us it is not our gender which represents the unknown but our own bodies. Reich (1949) argued that as young children we experience and store strong feelings and emotions in our musculature, particularly those linked to trauma and hurt. The body provides an internal and external map of our emotional history for those skilful enough to read it. For clients to take greater control over their lives, it becomes necessary to learn how to read or navigate the map their own body provides, as well as the imagination.

So far, the emphasis of this book has been on the application of imagery to help with deep-rooted psychological distress which is brought to the counselling room. However, imagery has also been used to work with clients who present with physical symptoms of illness and imagery work can also be used effectively to change or modify the physical symptoms themselves. We address the connections between imagery and bodily experience in five main areas:

- The use of imagery in relation to physical symptoms such as headaches, muscular pain, queasy or nauseous stomachs and sleeplessness, which are likely to have a psychosomatic basis. Many of these reactions only occur when the individual is under stress and managing stress more effectively may help to alleviate these symptoms. We will discuss ways in which imagery can be used to reduce or even remove these symptoms.
- We continue with the use of imagery work to make life more positive for individuals suffering from serious illness with a clearer physical basis, such as cancer.
- We give examples of ways to use imagery directly to help clients to learn to physically relax, even at times of stress and pressure.
- We examine ways in which breathing can be utilised to enhance the positive effects of imagery work.
- Finally we discuss some of the speculative notions of how imagery is mediated through the neural pathways of the brain.

Imagery and symptom relief

We use the word 'symptom' here to refer to physical discomfort that does not have a clear somatic basis and may be the product of muscular tension or a diminished immune system resulting from psychological distress. A wide range of conditions, such as headaches, neck, shoulder and back pain, bruxism, high blood pressure, insomnia, stomach pains, come into this category. These conditions, combined with excessive worry and anxiety, will maintain the body in a high state of arousal for prolonged periods of time which results in a wearing down of the body's coping mechanisms. Mason (2001) provides a number of relaxation exercises for reducing stress and also suggests a range of therapeutic visualisation techniques which the counsellor might find useful.

Clients can be encouraged to provide an image of the symptom itself, such as a headache or pain which the counsellor then works with directly. The example which follows does not come from the counselling room, but emerged from a chance meeting with a friend at work who appeared to be in a distressed state.

Eric:	Are you all right? You look as though you are in pain.
Colleague:	I've got a terrible migraine. I just don't know what to do with myself. I think I will have to go home.
Eric:	Would you like to try something that might help?
Colleague:	OK!
Eric:	If you had an image for your migraine, what would it look like?
Colleague:	It's like a metal cube.
Eric:	What colour is the cube?
Colleague:	It's a hard, metallic grey colour.
Eric:	Turn it round in your mind and have a good look at it. [pause] Now imagine that it is on my hand. [holding out hand] Can you do that?
Colleague:	Yes. [hesitantly]
Eric:	Now I am going to walk down the corridor holding the cube in the palm of my hand and it will seem to be getting smaller and smaller. [reaches a turn in the corridor] Now I am going to put it in my pocket [acts this out] and you can have it back any time you like. [disappears around the corner].

Working on the assumption that the migraine was serving some function for the colleague, the possibility of retrieving it was built in. It is important that the counsellor should not attempt to remove anything permanently from the client, even in imagination, as it swings the power dynamic in the counsellor's favour and places them in the role of expert. Throughout the therapeutic process, clients learn about the consequences of the choices they make in their lives, so to have a counsellor remove the possibility of choice can have a deleterious effect.

This particular interaction was brief, but the colleague reported later that the migraine had disappeared completely as the writer turned the corner. She recounted this to several other colleagues and the writer temporarily acquired the reputation of being something of a miracle worker! The important point is that the intervention was made with complete confidence, as if it were the most natural thing in the world.

Here is another example from a client who was experiencing a strong physical reaction to her anger:

Client:	I feel very angry today, I don't know why, it just started when I got up and there doesn't seem to be a reason.
Counsellor:	Where are you feeling this anger?
Client:	There is a tight lump, like a knot in my chest.
Counsellor:	Just take a few deep breaths and concentrate on this feeling . . . Can you describe it to me?
Client:	It's like a tight ball of wool.
Counsellor:	Does it have a colour?
Client:	It's red, bright red.
Counsellor:	I want you to cup your hands in front of you and keep breathing. Now imagine that the bright red ball of wool is in your hands. Can you do that?
Client:	Yes I think so . . . Oh here it is. It's a very tight ball . . . wound very tightly.

Counsellor:	Now look at it and imagine it beginning to shrink . . . so it is a tiny little red ball. [pause] Tell me how you are doing.
Client:	I'm breathing into it, not much is happening, I'm concentrating hard and . . . oh! It's getting smaller. Yes it's a little red ball now.
Counsellor:	I want you to give the ball to me, just place it in my hand. [stretches out hand] OK! I'm putting this shrunken ball of wool on my coffee table here. It can stay here as long as you want, it isn't hurting me or anything else and it is safe here. You can leave it here, but if you do want it back, all you need to do is ask me. So you have control of it. How are you feeling now?
Client:	[Breathes deeply] The tight feeling has gone, it's funny, I feel quite calm. I can leave that little ball with you as long as I want?
Counsellor:	Yes.
Client:	I don't ever want it back!

When the client returned for her next session, she reported that she had often thought of the little ball of red wool on the coffee table but had not felt the tension and the angry feelings associated with it. She also remarked happily that she felt free from the unexplained anger she had so often felt in the past.

Another client reported experiencing anxious, racing thoughts that constantly interrupted her sleep causing problems with coping during the day. The counsellor was able to use a quick intervention that helped restore her healthy sleeping pattern. Coincidentally, she came up with a similar image involving balls of wool.

Counsellor:	Can you describe what it feels like in your head with all these thoughts racing around?
Client:	I feel very woolly, everything is a jumble. All connected, there is no beginning and no end.
Counsellor:	You talk about this feeling of wooliness. Is there an image you have for what's happening?
Client:	[pause] Well, it's a bit like a large basket, full of balls of wool – all different shapes and colours, different thicknesses and somehow all the balls have become tangled. When I was a girl, I used to sit with my grandmother and hold the wool between my hands like this [holds out hands about 12 inches apart] while she wound it into balls.
Counsellor:	When you think of that memory, how do you feel?
Client:	Happy and cosy. Safe, I enjoyed those times.
Counsellor:	Maybe we can use it to help you sort out your woolly thoughts. Begin to relax now, allow your breath to flow freely, deeply, and be aware of the rhythm of your breath. Now begin to let the tension go, feel yourself letting go and relaxing . . . Now imagine the large basket with all its different types of wool. All its many colours, the balls all different sizes, some wound loosely and some tightly. Now look closely at that basket. It's in a very big tangle. All the balls are mixed up together and there is a large muddle in the basket. Can you see it?
Client:	Yes.

Counsellor: Before the balls of wool can be used, they need to be separated and sorted into wool sizes. As you look at the basket begin to look for the ends of wool, see if you can pull any balls out of the muddle. Take your time and tell me when you have done all you can.

Client: [long pause] There is still quite a muddle in the basket, but I have pulled out quite a few balls of different coloured wool.

Counsellor: What do you want to do with them now?

Client: I'm sorting them by colour and putting them in smaller baskets. That's much neater.

Counsellor: Look back at the basket now and see if there is anything else you can do to sort out the muddle. Do you need to wind up some balls? Have any become unravelled? Look around and see if there is something you can use to wind the wool. Take your time and tell me when you have done all you can.

Client: I've been able to separate the balls now. I wound up some of the wool to make balls but some of it had become just too tangled. I have decided to cut it off and throw it away.

Counsellor: What's in the basket now?

Client: It's full of balls of wool that are ready to be used. There are now several baskets, one big and a few small, all with wool in. The small ones are all the same colours but the big one has a mixture of colours and thickness of wool.

Counsellor: As you look at these baskets make a note of how you feel. Become aware of your breathing again and hold onto these images of tidy balls of wool. When your thoughts are racing in bed, you can conjure up this image and know that the thoughts that have been captured will be safe until the morning. When you feel ready gently come back to the room.

In later sessions, the client reported that her sleep had been helped a great deal by recreating this scene in imagination before going off to sleep and subsequently she began to unpack specific issues related to the recurring anxieties and the underlying causes, something of a breakthrough in her struggle for greater self-awareness and control.

In this example, it is likely that the use of the imagery itself induced a relaxed state, with a lowered level of internal arousal and a resulting reduction in muscular tension, causing the necessary physical conditions for the symptoms of anxiety to disappear. Once the client had gained a significant measure of control over her own internal processes, she felt more confident about a more thorough-going analysis of the underlying reasons for the condition.

Using creative visualisation for healing

In a little known, but intriguing book, Shattock (1979) reports on his attempts to use creative visualisation to heal various physical ailments he suffered from. A naval man by profession, Admiral Shattock seems an unlikely practitioner and advocate for the use of imagery for self-healing. The book describes the methods by which he removed fibrous growths from his hip, reduced the size of his prostate gland and removed a polyp from his nose, all through creative visualisation techniques. He did this, among other interventions, by imagining processes such as restricting blood flow to unwanted tissue and increasing blood flow to encourage white blood cells to scavenge unwanted cells. His sceptical GP was surprised by the extent that Shattock was able to effect these changes. He had been trained in Buddhist meditation and had developed the ability to concentrate deeply for prolonged periods. He had also carefully checked the exact anatomical processes that were required to bring about the desired physical changes. The approach he adopted was specifically related to the exact physiology of the body and therefore more literal than the approaches to healing that follow in this section.

Adopting and adapting the use of imagery and creative visualisation for physical healing was popularised by Simonton et al. (1980) with their book, *Getting Well Again*. The authors were practising oncologists in the USA and therefore their clinical status gave them additional credibility. This book caught the popular imagination because it held out the possibility of a self-generated cure for cancer from respected medical practitioners. They emphasised the importance of working on both the experience of stress and the epistemological beliefs of patients with cancers. They argued that stress weakens the ability of the immune system to stave off disease and to counteract this they encouraged patients to relax three times daily and in addition to use images that would contribute to the removal of cancer cells from the body. They provide one example of a patient who imagined their white blood cells as sharks that were busily consuming the invading cancer cells. They made the assumption that patient-generated imagery would be the most effective in the treatment programme. They initially encouraged patients to use aggressive forms of imagery to help them combat the sense of helplessness that often accompanies a diagnosis of a possibly terminal illness. They modified this approach as some research participants reported feeling uncomfortable with aggression. They reported from their research some remarkable examples of remission from cancer, but the most significant outcome appeared to be that patients who used imagery lived longer and enjoyed a better quality of life than those who only used conventional forms of treatment. Visualisation and imagery techniques combined with 'conventional' therapies tended to have greater success than conventional therapy alone.

Naparstek (1995) uses similar approaches to the use of creative visualisation and guided imagery in healing. She describes the application of imagery techniques to improve general health and well-being, such as increasing energy levels, strengthening the immune system, relieving depression, expressing grief and understanding psychological problems. She also offers imagery for dealing with common physical complaints such as headaches and allergies. Like Simonton et al. (1980) she suggests that the most effective forms of imagery for self-healing are client-generated.

A student from South East Asia who developed cancer, recounted how she visited a traditional healer in her mother country who taught her a self-management technique he called 'internal Kung Fu'. The process involved imagining a flow of energy around the body, including the affected parts with a view to diminishing the cancer in those areas. She reported increased energy levels and a renewed zest for life. This internal movement of energy is similar to the practice of Qi Gong which is a central element of the T'ai Chi movement systems. Brigham's account (1994) provides a lively, fascinating discussion on the use of Qi Gong for the healing of serious physical illnesses. In her work, *Imagery for Getting Well*, she describes imagery applied to a wide range of physical disorders, emphasising the importance of relaxation and the reduction of stress to improve and strengthen the functioning of the auto-immune system. She also helpfully provides a substantial number of carefully crafted scripts and themes for working on specific conditions, as well as describing often moving case histories of her client's recovery from illness, many of whom had been diagnosed as terminal by the medical establishment.

A further application of imagery in relation to physical illness is in the reduction of the experience of pain, and imagery sequences to help patients alleviate their pain is provided by both Simonton et al. (1980) and Brigham (1994). We discuss the research evidence for using imagery techniques to combat physical illness in Chapter 9, which overall is positive. If imagery can have a positive effect on the physical condition of the body, it seems likely to have positive outcomes for addressing the psychological issues that are brought to the counselling room.

Imagery and relaxation

Racing, uncontrollable or compulsive thought patterns appear to play an important part in the lives of individuals who experience psychological discomfort. All of us will have experienced waking up in the early hours, with a mind full of thoughts, feelings and worries. Thinking, particularly worry, tends to raise the body's general level of arousal and if this pattern becomes chronic, it can have a debilitating effect on the physical body even causing illness or disease. One way of reducing such high levels of arousal, is to learn to relax and we explore the relationship between imagery and relaxation in the next section.

We previously explained how it is helpful to encourage a client to relax in order to encourage the flow of imagery and have provided brief instructions for relaxation at the beginning of a guided imagery journey or a script. Once an individual or a group become accustomed to these processes they learn to relax almost immediately. The act of paying attention to images is however relaxing in its own right. In a virtuous circle, relaxation can be used to facilitate imagery and imagery can be used to facilitate relaxation.

In our experience, some clients are too tense to sit still even for a short period and it may be appropriate to take them through a more prolonged relaxation procedure before introducing imagery techniques into the session. There are a number of different ways to encourage relaxation and here we provide an approach that has proved successful with the majority of our clients and trainee groups.

The preamble is similar to the initial instructions at the beginning of a session of guided imagery: 'Sit upright, with your feet placed firmly on the floor, with the hands resting lightly on the thighs'. This is probably the optimal position for relaxation, because it allows the breath to move freely. However, if the client prefers a different position, such as lying on the floor or slumping in a comfortable chair, then it is best to allow the choice.

The voice of the counsellor is an important instrument to facilitate relaxation. A lower register appears to be helpful and it is important to talk at a slower rate than you would in normal conversation and to pause between phrases and sentences. Counsellors and counsellors-in-training would do well to practise their vocal technique and solicit feedback on its effectiveness as an instrument. One format is to set up triads in a training group where one tries out the technique, one acts as the client and the third is an observer. This provides the possibility of feedback for the trainee from two viewpoints.

With experience, it is possible to improvise and adapt the procedure to suit the needs of the client, but here we provide a basic script. We suggest placing the emphasis on each of the syllables, words or phrases that are printed in bold.

Counsellor: Make yourself comfortable in your chair. . . . Place your feet flat on the floor and your hands on your thighs. . . . Take some deeper breaths . . . and as you breathe out, have the sense of **letting go**. . . . It is helpful to **close your eyes** . . . and if they are already closed, imagine that you are closing them again. . . . Right now you might be aware of faint noises in the building. [or refer to any noises in the environment] . . . If there are any more noises of any kind, you will still be able to **relax and let go**. . . . It's just energy in the environment. You may be aware of the sound of my voice, and curious about what I might say next. . . . Be aware of your breathing and the air passing through your nostrils, . . . a relaxed expansion and contraction of the ribcage as the body breathes itself. You may even have the sense that the body is being breathed by the wider energy field in the room. . . . Become aware of the temperature in the room . . . and the feel of the air against any exposed skin. . . . As the muscles in the face **relax**, the muscles around the eyes and mouth **release and let go**. . . . The jaws **relax,** . . . and have the sense that the neck and shoulders are opening and the head finds a comfortable position in which to rest. . . . Right now, you may be aware of the feel of your body

> against the chair you are sitting in or floor you are lying on. . . . As your arms and legs **relax and extend**, . . . your stomach **relaxes** and your breathing **becomes even more relaxed**. . . . Right now, become aware of the taste in your mouth and the unique smell of the room.

If the client is experienced in using relaxation and has established a trusting relationship, you may wish to continue as follows:

> As the body continues to move **down** . . . **down** . . . **down** . . . **down** . . . **down**, **deeper down** . . . **down** . . . **deep** . . . **deep** . . . **down**, all the way to the centre of the earth. Perhaps moving down to a deeper level of relaxation than you've known for some time. . . . Knowing that **this is a safe place to relax and let go**. . . . It is as if the body is suspended in a warm, liquid medium. . . . [long pause]

Otherwise, bring the relaxation to a close by saying:

> When it feels right for you, begin to **come back to the room**. . . . Breathe a little more deeply. . . . Perhaps begin to move your fingers and toes. When you feel ready, **open your eyes** [if still closed] and give yourself a good stretch and yawn if you want to. . . . Take a moment to hold on to an awareness of what it is like to be more relaxed and bring that feeling back with you into the room.

If the phrases in bold are emphasised during the relaxation they can over time act as embedded commands (Grinder and Bandler, 1981). The emphasis can be achieved by either saying them slightly louder or with a lowered voice or even both. The theory is that the embedded command is heard at a low level of awareness (and therefore defensiveness) and the client 'obeys' the command because they are in a heightened state of suggestibility during relaxation. Some might describe this technique as manipulative, but the intention is benign and the manipulation strategically therapeutic with the consent of the client or group themselves.

It is useful to ask for feedback on their experience of the relaxation. A small proportion of clients report an *increase* in tension at the end of the relaxation. It is possible that these individuals are simply unused to tuning in to internal sensory data and thus forced to become more aware of the degree of tension they experience for the first time. It is worth offering this possibility to them. All clients we have worked with have improved their ability to relax over time and with practice. Some clients can relax very deeply and do not readily come out of the relaxed state and may even ask if they have been hypnotised. Actually the difference between deep relaxation and hypnosis remains unclear and it is possible that for most people, hypnosis is simply a deep state of relaxation. You might include suggestions towards the end of the relaxation to the effect that the client will enjoy a good night's sleep or have a significant dream, if this is appropriate to the stage the therapy has reached. If these suggestions do nothing more than leave the client in a relaxed state, this will be of substantial benefit. The experience of relaxation will have ameliorated the physical and psychological effects of stress for a short period of time, reminding the body of a more natural, calm inner state. This memory can then be used as a focus to reinforce future learning.

Breathing 'into' the image

Another technique which further links the process of guided imagery and bodily sensation is to encourage the client to *breathe into* particular images that have been generated. This can be used in therapeutic contexts, such as when the client reports a blockage or tension in part of the body, an experience of a strong feeling or emotion, or where there is a physical sense of energy moving in the body. Breathing into a feeling or part of the body tends to have the effect of amplifying the experience as if a volume switch had been turned up. The client can gain a better understanding of the meaning of the experience and the extent to which it has an effect on their lives. For clients who are in depressed or avoidant states, damped down or repressed feeling can be brought into awareness – a vague sense of irritation can be experienced as anger, a vague but a mild sense of happiness might be experienced as joy. It is as if by daring to enter into the experience more fully, the client can learn to explore and identify the feeling, presenting the possibility of recognising and expressing it more authentically in the future.

This client came into counselling to learn how to handle his fiery, uncontrollable outbursts and loss of temper, which in the past had actually resulted in self-harm. This excerpt is taken from a client–counsellor exchange which involved an examination of the physical sensation experienced when he was on the verge of losing his temper.

Counsellor: How does it feel when you're beginning to lose your temper?
Client: I get a tightness across my chest and then suddenly I can't control myself, I need to hurt myself.
Counsellor: Can you feel anything now?
Client: Yes, yes I can. The tightness is right across my chest. I can't think what the trigger could be, but it is there. Wait a minute, I know what it is. I feel irritated because the coffee table is untidy.
Counsellor: OK, stay with the feeling, breathe into it. Try to exaggerate it, allow the tightness to be there. How does it feel now?
Client: It's very tight. I feel I need to punch or hit something to hurt myself and then the feeling will go [hands clench into fists and face looks strained].
Counsellor: Keep breathing into the feeling and see what happens.
Client: [after a few moments]. It's subsiding now, I can look at the coffee table and I don't feel irritated. It's completely gone. That's just not logical. I can't understand how that could happen but I feel quite peaceful now.

> *Counsellor*: Now, when you next have that feeling, take a few moments and breathe into it, just as you have done here. See if you can control it before it erupts into an angry outburst.

The following week he identified coming home to an untidy house as a trigger for the anger. He had been reluctant to attempt the breathing exercise as he couldn't understand the logic behind it. However, he did try it when he felt the anger welling up and managed to release the pressure and avoid his usual outburst. Whenever he felt his anger welling up he continued to practise breathing with good results. At the end of the counselling sessions he said, 'I have believed I can handle things through violence because it is acceptable, but actually it isn't and I don't have to give in to violent behaviour'.

It isn't necessary or desirable to always end a guided imagery journey or a counselling session on what might be conventionally regarded as a positive note. However, it isn't difficult to engineer this if this seems appropriate to the counsellor and in the interests of the client's capacity to handle the coming week. If the client has worked through a difficult issue or surmounted an obstacle in the course of an imagery journey, they will often spontaneously report feelings of exhilaration and elation, and this can be built on when discussing strategies for behaviour change.

> *Counsellor*: Where exactly do you feel this excitement in your body?
> *Client*: It's like a warm feeling in my chest.
> *Counsellor*: Stay with that feeling and have the sense of breathing into it. It's as if you are increasing the feeling. . . . Now have the sense that, as you breathe into the feeling, it is expanding to fill the whole of your body, filling your head, your arms, and your legs.
> *Client*: This is amazing. I haven't felt so energised for a long time.
> *Counsellor*: OK, when you are ready, begin to come out of the imagery, but try to hold on to those feelings, and recall them if you feel tired or de-energised during the coming week.

What's happening in the brain

There is a popular notion that imagery is a 'right brain activity' based on the assumption that the separate hemispheres of the frontal cortex of the brain each have different functions and that imagery is mediated in the right cerebral hemisphere in contrast to verbal, linguistic activity which is mediated in the left cerebral hemisphere. Other functions are often ascribed to each of the hemispheres and distinctions made between so-called 'left brain activities' such as language and logical thinking and 'right brain activities' such as visual imagery, spatial awareness, intuition, creativity and holistic thinking. Individuals might be described as 'left brain thinkers' or 'right brain thinkers' according to their preferred mode of relating to the world (Springer and Deutsch, 1998).

These early ideas emerged from experiments with epileptic patients who had had the connections between the two hemispheres, the corpus callosum, cut in order to reduce the debilitating effects of seizures. In this condition, it was noted that visual information presented to the right visual field which is processed in the left hemisphere could not be recognised. Verbal information presented to the left visual field and thence to the right hemisphere could not be understood either. These split brain studies were influential in developing the still common popular notion of left and right brain activities. However, as Solms and Turnbull (2002) point out, generalising from experiments with patients who already had problems with their brains is intrinsically problematic and that, in terms of anatomical structure, the two hemispheres are virtually identical and that, 'different parts of the different hemispheres are recruited into complex functional systems' (Solms and Turnbull, 2002: 244).

The experience of 'seeing' internally generated visual imagery is qualitatively different from the experience of what we see through the eye and there is no neurological reason to presume that internally generated imagery is mediated in the same way as external vision. In the construction of internal imagery, it is probable that information is being drawn from the memory data banks. In an early discussion of mental imagery, Pylyshyn (1973) argued that an image was more like description than a picture and that imagery was largely conceptual and drawn from memory, rather than being sensory or pictorial in nature, putting a question mark over the notion of 'in the mind's eye'. At present, there is no way of proving or disproving this hypothesis, but the reported act of imaging does appear to engage several areas in both hemispheres and specifically involves connections to areas that are known to be critical for emotion, such as the amygdala (Aggleton, 1992).

The neurophysiology of what is happening in the brain during the process of generating imagery is still uncertain. Based on the reports of individuals who have taken part in guided imagery, there appears to be two contrasting patterns of experience. During guided imagery, the client reports feeling relaxed, feelings appear to emerge more freely and there is a greater bodily awareness of these feelings. This contrasts with the experience of anxiety, worry and compulsive thinking that often involves internal verbal activity. This latter pattern is often accompanied with the symptoms of what we commonly call stress. Given these two contrasting patterns of experience, it is understandable that the notion of the split brain with different functions of the left and right hemispheres was and is appealing.

In this chapter we have explored a range of connections between imagery as it is experienced in guided imagery and processes that are happening in the body. Guided imagery is one way of coming to an understanding of these mind/body connections and opens up possibilities for a more integrated approach to well-being and personal development. In the next chapter we examine the research evidence for the therapeutic value of the use of imagery.

9

How Do We Know it Works?

The ultimate statistic in the world of the self is not the many, nor even the few, but a statistic in which N = 1, and that one is you, or I. This does not mean that you or the I dwells in isolation in a separate world. The self and the other are closely bound together. But the final repository of meaning is within each person as a separate self.

(Arthur Jersild, 1955: 134)

It's like magic. (female client aged 31)

Many of our clients have expressed a similar sense of wonderment after their first encounter with guided imagery. The impact in terms of psychological insight, temporary or long-lasting relief from symptoms such as stress, pain and anxiety have been recorded in the case histories we have reported in earlier chapters. But evidence that the use of imagery as a therapeutic tool has an impact, does not necessarily mean that it is making a contribution to the client's long-term improvement or well-being. Through the use of imagery, a client may report the experience of being relaxed for the first time in years, or feel 'spaced out', or enjoy an 'oceanic feeling'. Invariably, the reported power of the experience appears to be enhanced not diminished with further practice, but the process by which the change process occurs, if it occurs, needs to be carefully and systematically researched.

The choice of research paradigm depends on the questions which are being asked and we would argue that both quantitative and qualitative methodologies have an important part to play in the evaluation of the impact of guided imagery work on therapeutic progress. Qualitative research can draw out rich, thick descriptions of the psychological processes at play, not only for the client, but in the counsellor–client relationship, when guided imagery forms a part of the therapeutic process. The systematic recording and analysing of such accounts go a long way towards illuminating what may be sometimes seen as a mysterious or magical process and therefore sidelined by sceptics who use the absence of research evidence to suggest that these techniques might in some way damage clients' welfare. As a profession, we are bound by our code of ethics and duty of care to clients to produce a robust evidence base for what works and why in the therapeutic process. What constitutes 'evidence' can be debated, but we would argue that both quantitative and qualitative approaches have their place in the researcher's tool-kit (McLeod, 2003). However, a high proportion of published quantitative studies employ self-report questionnaires which are notoriously susceptible to respondents answering questions in a way they assume will please the researcher or to create a positive impression of themselves. Some outcome studies do use externally observable or verifiable sources of data, such as reduction in or ending of medication, or weight loss/gain in the treatment of eating disorder, which are more in keeping with the positivist traditions of quantitative research.

Research using control groups

Most of the research into the outcomes of the use of guided imagery in its various forms using control groups, comes from medicine and nursing (Achterberg, 1985; Graham, 1990; Brigham, 1994). Arbuthnot et al. (2001) provide an impressive review of the outcome studies from the use of a range of forms of guided imagery. These include improving the rate and extent of healing following surgery or serious illness, reducing stress and infectious illness and the management of chronic pain. In the psychotherapeutic context, Arbuthnot et al. review the evidence which indicates positive effects of the use of imagery in relation to stress, panic attacks, post-traumatic stress disorder, attaining treatment goals in brief psychodynamic psychotherapy, improving complex motor skills and performance, and the ability to alter mood at will.

In the research literature to date, there is little evidence to suggest that the use of guided imagery is in any way damaging to clients. The one area which remains problematic, however, is the use of guided imagery by therapists to enable clients to recall or even re-experience past memories which appear to have generated both real and imagined memories of childhood abuse, particularly sexual abuse. Certainly, our experience is that clients who are aware and have always been aware that they have been sexually abused, gain a great deal from the use of guided imagery as part of their therapy. However, none of our clients or trainees has had a recovered memory of sexual abuse as a result of going through the process. Individual clients will sometimes make an association between imagery they generate with events from the past but they often regard this as positive.

Arbuthnot et al. (2001) discuss in detail the possibility of harming the client by using guided imagery and conclude that there is no good reason which would contraindicate the use of imagery in psychotherapeutic contexts, with the caveat that care should be taken with the use of imagery involving the evocation of 'real-life' memories, which may be too painful for the client to experience. We return to this issue in Chapter 10 where we discuss the caveats around using guided imagery in the counselling context.

An overlapping review of the quantitative research on the outcomes of using imagery is provided by Heinschel (2002). This review provides evidence of the positive outcomes of using imagery to treat anxiety, the alleviation of pain, the length of hospital stay following medical interventions and immune function, such as blood cortisol levels, natural killer cell function and the production of haemoglobin. In the studies reviewed, there appeared to be no evidence that working with imagery did clients any harm; a finding which confirms our professional experience over a number of years.

Qualitative research

Having reviewed these quantitative studies, Heinschel (2002) goes on to describe her own qualitative research which provides a phenomenological analysis of Interactive Guided Imagery, a form of guided imagery along the lines of the techniques we describe in Chapters 2 and 3. Her work provides an insight into ten clients' experience. It appeared that although the content of a guided imagery journey will vary substantially from client to client, the nature of the process was similar across a diverse client group. The thematic analysis of the tapes of semi-structured interviews revealed six main themes, which closely matches an analysis of our own experience. The themes were:

- the clients lived the imagery experience
- the involvement of a 'non-ordinary' state of consciousness
- the client regarded the guide as essential to derive full benefit from the experience
- the client–guide relationship had to be trusting and respectful
- factors affecting the Interactive Guided Imagery experience included the guide's demonstration of competence, establishing trust, rapport and being relaxed and patient
- clients were able to point to significant evidence of impact.

Heinschel's (2002) study went beyond simple accounts of case history experience by using current methods of thematic analysis rather than drawing out the common elements from case histories. However, this is not to devalue the importance of data from single and multiple case histories based on clinical experience and we go on to consider case histories in the latter part of this chapter.

Integrative research: the combined method approach

In a project that combined both quantitative and qualitative methods, Hall (1983) guided individual adults through a series of imagery journeys. He then gave a group of adults and a group of adolescents the same themes in a scripted form. This was done over a period of weeks. The same elements within the imagery journeys were elaborated within each theme. The elements were evaluated using their own personal constructs (Kelly, 1955). The participants were able to ascribe human qualities to the elements, and they all produced a coherent set of personal attributes that ran through all the themes, suggesting a consistent underlying structure to the imagery. A whole series of images might relate to a single emotional issue and conversely individual images related to several emotional issues, lending support to Freud's notions of overdetermination and condensation which he applied to dreams. There was also strong support for a high proportion of images relating to a defended–undefended dimension, which was also identified by Assagioli (1965).

An interesting outcome from the 'exploring the body' imagery journey, was the perception of the throat, which was consistently perceived as being tense. The body therapists who have developed Reich's (1949) work, such as Lowen (1975) and Kelley (1974), suggest a link between emotional repression and physical sites in the body and that the blocking of emotional experience is often accompanied by tension in the throat. They also see the belly as the locus of fear and this image was also perceived as being apprehensive and tense by the respondents in our study. Another connection between the physical body and imagery experience came out of the bird in a cage narrative. The cage generally appeared in the defended grouping of constructs and three volunteers reported that they could actually feel the cage as a tension within their own bodies; the bird correlated highly with 'myself'. This could be interpreted as part of the self represented by the bird feeling trapped inside a highly defended part of the self represented by the cage.

Good moments in counselling and psychotherapy

It would be insufficient to limit the collection of research evidence to so-called objective studies on the effectiveness of guided imagery in counselling and ignore the voices of clients and counsellors themselves. Mahrer and Nadler (1986) write about 'good moments in psychotherapy', when both the client and the counsellor consider that a particular part of the therapeutic process has been especially helpful. They argue that these descriptive categories provide sound evidence of the impact of therapeutic interventions on the helping process. We support Mahrer and Nadler's view and we offer the clients' voice concerning their experience of guided imagery and the ways in which they considered it to be of importance to them in their personal development.

We have provided a number of examples when the client regarded the experience of imagery as stimulating a major personal breakthrough. Many of the examples we have provided earlier were described by the clients themselves as pivotal in their development. In a few reports the client felt the initial experience disturbed their habitual ways of viewing experience, but at a later stage came to understand that the imagery was working for them positively.

The next example shows a dramatic experience of breakthrough which emerged from a discussion of a spontaneously generated image. It was closely related to bodily experience and involved the use of breathing to heighten the sensory experience. The client was a physically and psychologically tense person who had extreme difficulty in expressing feelings. As he talked about his inability to express these feelings, he reported a powerful feeling of tightness in his chest that was becoming increasingly painful.

Counsellor: Close your eyes for a moment and breathe into that feeling.
Client: It's becoming even more painful.
Counsellor: If you had an image for this pain, what would it be?
[The client suddenly sat upright.]
Client: That's amazing, I've got this image of a large stake going straight through my chest. It's enormous, the point is coming out through my back and the front end goes out a long way and the end is as thick as a tree trunk. The weight of it is really painful.
Counsellor: What do you want to do?
Client: I'd like you to hold the thick end and take some of the weight.
Counsellor: OK! I've got hold of it now [simulates this action even though the client has his eyes closed].
Client: That's a relief. I think I would like you to try to pull it out. Don't do it all at once, I think that would be too painful. Just try pulling a little. [There followed a series of pulls which the client controlled and making groaning sounds with each imagined movement of the stake. He reported the final moment as the stake was pulled out as an mixture of pain and joy and he sat breathing deeply for several minutes.]

This was a very vivid experience for both the client and the counsellor. In subsequent sessions he showed an increased willingness to disclose feelings and reported that he was now enjoying voluntarily and spontaneously opening up to people in his life. He also reported a significant reduction in bodily tension, particularly in the chest area. This example illustrates the interconnections between visual imagery, bodily experience and the use of the breath to heighten sensation as well as demonstrating behaviour change as a direct result of the experience.

Here is another example which illustrates the way the counsellor can use the integration of imagery, bodily experience and breathing. This client presented as a result of feeling overcome by extreme feelings of anxiety and concerns over her relationship with her daughter. She wanted to find some measure of relief from the physical sensations she was experiencing.

Counsellor: Can you describe what you're feeling right now?

Client: Yes, it's like a fluttering in my stomach, it's horrible.

Counsellor: Well, instead of ignoring it, try breathing into it. Take some deep breaths and breathe deeply into the feeling in your stomach. [Silence and a look of concentration on client's face.] Can you describe what's happening?

Client: Yes, they feel like butterflies, beautiful butterflies! As I breathe they are settling and spreading their wings, they're so beautiful. I AM A BEAUTIFUL BUTTERFLY! [A look of wonder came over the client's face.] I can't believe it but I feel so much calmer now.

The next session the client arrived looking more serene than she had appeared before and she volunteered the following comment:

Client: I felt amazing as I left and ever since I just imagine these beautiful creatures with their wings spread in the sunshine and I feel fine. I'm not afraid of the feelings of anxiety anymore.

The following examples are taken from just a few of our case histories and provide illustrations of the range of imagery that has been reported by clients as having produced a significant shift in their progress. These involved images that were spontaneously generated during counselling and reflect the rich diversity of the clients' social, philosophical and in some cases, religious approach to life.

Client 1: After the visualisation I felt a weight was lifted from me and I feel free at last. I think it's incredible. I didn't have to destroy the monsters. Now they have no power over me, after all this time.

Client 2: When I get an image I can work with, like taking the weight off my chest and shrinking it, I begin to feel more in control.

Client 3: Now I have an image for the feelings they are not so powerful and I'm not frightened.

Client 4: I use the image of the water in front of me as it gives me space inside when my resources are pressed. It's friendly, oxygenating. It's like the breath of life.

Client 5: When I'm consumed with anxious thoughts, I imagine my mind as a 'sim card'. I simply see myself putting a new 'sim card' into my head and I feel less pressurised almost immediately.

Client 6:   I love to use the image of the White Rabbit to diffuse fraught work situations. The rabbit rushes around on automatic pilot, looking at his watch anxiously as he thinks he is late. 'Oh my fur and whiskers!' he says.

Client 7:   When I think of the image of Jesus Christ lying asleep flat out in the boat in the raging storm, my problems simply vanish from my mind.

Client 8:   When I'm pressurised at work, I imagine my head being sprinkled with clean pure water from a beautiful golden flask.

Client 9:   When I'm filled with negative thoughts about my pending exam results, I can now visualise these as a jangled picture of wires and bulbs flashing in my head. My remedy is to turn the switch off in my head, the lights go out, and the worries melt away.

Client 10:   Once in our counselling sessions, we did some guided imagery to help release some of the anger I was feeling. This began by closing my eyes and imagining climbing up the long and winding path around a volcano, slowly feeling the grass underfoot gradually change to stony ground. Whilst doing this I could feel myself imaging the volcano's heat become my own. We also stood up and began to stamp around to help release some of the feelings building up inside me. Things that had been difficult over the last few days were at the forefront of my mind and I felt myself wanting to get to the top so I could let go of some of these feelings. Gradually the stomping got louder and harder and I shook myself and let out shouts which became more forceful as I tried to release each feeling as it came to me. This carried on for a while until I felt I had released much of this anger, and then I began to feel calmer and sat back down.

It was quite good to do this with someone else, in that I find it difficult to give myself permission to express these feelings, and I have a lot of angry feelings! To have someone else with me validated the experience. At first it felt a bit silly to use this imagery but this was soon forgotten and I got quite into it. I enjoyed the experience so much that afterwards at home when feeling angry, I would use a rolling pin and bash my bed really quite ferociously at times to get some of this anger out. This was very helpful and was triggered off really by the volcano imagery. I still use this now instead of sitting stewing with these feelings, and find it very releasing.

The research regarding the effectiveness of guided imagery in counselling and therapeutic situations is still at best fragmentary and plagued by the intrinsic problems of participant self-report. However, taken together with evidence from the research studies reported in Chapter 8 on the relationship between imagery and healing, we begin to see a more compelling case unfold. If guided imagery in the therapeutic context can be used creatively to increase client self-management and self-healing then the process needs to be seriously researched.

The study and evaluation of any form of psychotherapeutic intervention is complex and sometimes slippery, but we must continue to push the methodological boundaries which currently constrain the limited evidence we have. The literature on guided imagery is full of inspiring, transpersonal and spiritual theory with claims which may never be amenable to conventional research investigation. On the other hand, there is a growing body of evidence from academic sources to suggest that guided imagery is at the very least a helpful intervention in counselling and can have a beneficial impact on the resolution of troubling symptoms such as anxiety, depression and blocked feelings which blight the lives of many of our clients.

10

Ethical Considerations: Contraindications and Health Warnings

This is dangerous!
How do I know where this will lead?
Guided imagery can't surely be suitable for use with all clients?

These statements are a distillation of the concerns raised by counsellors in practice, counsellor educators and counsellor trainees and as such demand attention. We alluded earlier to the not uncommon view that the use of guided imagery in therapy is potentially dangerous because it may revive memories of traumatic events and that only a specialist should work with these memories. This warning is applied particularly to the recovery of memories of childhood sexual abuse. Some professionals suggest that the early career counsellor should not meddle in high-risk activities and leave imagery work to their more experienced colleagues. We would agree that the novice counsellor should only use techniques for which they have been properly trained. However, we do not agree with the view that the use of imagery is any more dangerous to the client's psychological well-being than any other approach used in counselling if the guidelines provided in this book are properly followed. It is not the technique *per se* which is risky but the techniques in the hands of an incompetent counsellor. It is, however, necessary to consider the possible contraindications, health warnings and ethical considerations related to the use of imagery in therapeutic contexts.

The issue of recovered memories of childhood sexual abuse has been a topic of professional and legal debate for a number of years. On the one hand it is argued that guided imagery will increase the probability that there will be a recovered memory of early trauma and on the other it is claimed that guided imagery can be used to implant a false memory because of the heightened suggestibility of the client (False Memory Syndrome). These claims related to false memory, whether fictitious or distorted, are difficult to prove but the evidence that some reports of memories of sexual abuse appear to be false and to have been constructed by the procedures used by the counsellor or therapist, seem incontrovertible.

There have been dramatic cases where parents have been prosecuted on the basis of a childhood recovered memory unearthed in therapy, which have subsequently been demonstrated as impossible to have actually occurred. However, a survey conducted by the British Psychological Society (1995) concluded that there was only limited support for False Memory Syndrome. At the extremes, some counsellors take the view that all recovered memories are genuine while others would argue that many have been manipulated in some way by the counsellor or knowingly or unknowingly constructed by the client.

Whether clients have or have not experienced sexual or other forms of abuse or trauma in their background does not seem relevant to a discussion of contraindications of using imagery as a therapeutic tool. Every client brings with them narratives of hurt and pain, and the antecedents may be real or imagined. The counsellor's role is to support the client's interrogation, understanding and reintegration of these narratives into their lives in order to move forward with confidence. It is in this understanding and reintegration process that the use of guided imagery can make a significant impact. It is clear from the case histories we present that the imagery journeys very rarely relate to what might be called real-life events.

Undergoing the experience of guided imagery has been compared with hypnosis, opening the possibility of distortion through suggestion. All of us are suggestible to some degree and there will be a normal distribution of suggestibility across the population, while we all become more suggestible in a relaxed state. Grinder and Bandler (1981) maintain that all communication involves suggestion which can be reinforced by the way language is used. Teachers are trained to use positive rather than negative language in order to manage behaviour in large groups of students. Relationships between people who have a trusting, intimate psychological connection are more likely to be highly suggestible and prone to believe and act on what the other says.

There is no existing research evidence which suggests that the use of guided imagery in therapeutic settings will produce recovered memories. Arbuthnot et al. (2001) use the term 'metaphoric imagery' for the approach to imagery we describe to distinguish it from the use of imagery to go back in time and remember events from childhood. It is this latter approach that generates recovered memories. This is a source of confusion as both could be described as guided imagery since both procedures involve a guide and the use of imagery. The use of imagery for remembering events in the past is not recommended here, though it may be helpful for some clients. The use of the word 'fantasy' might be a better term to describe the activity we are encouraging (Hall, 1983; Hall et al., 1990) to distinguish it from memory imagery, but guided imagery is the term that is most widely used in the literature and that most professionals will be familiar with.

Arbuthnot et al. (2001) conclude a thorough review of the theory and research in the area by recommending the use of metaphoric imagery as a means of minimising the possibility of psychological damage to the client, given that the outcomes are consistently positive. Indeed, Courtois (2001) argues that it is not imagery *per se* that produces memory distortion but leading questioning techniques on the part of the therapist, which implants suggestions in the client.

This phenomenon is exacerbated with clients who are suggestible, prone to dissociate and have strong approval needs. Courtois further argues that most of the psychotherapeutic techniques that involve remembered events, such as dealing with traumatic experiences and symptom reduction are not prone to memory distortion and that the potential dangers of using both memory and metaphoric imagery in psychotherapeutic contexts is exaggerated.

Enns (2001) suggests that a careful assessment can reveal if issues of recovered memory are likely to occur. A history of traumatic experience and gaps in memory for past experience she claims would be indicators of caution in relation to the use of imagery techniques. She provides support for the notion of informing the client about the possibilities for memory distortion, which would not be necessary for the forms of guided imagery we discuss here, as they do not involve memory retrieval.

Reference was made in the previous section to the issue of clients who are prone to dissociate and a further warning that is given in relation to the use of guided imagery is that some clients may dissociate while they are going through the experience. The term dissociation tends to be used loosely, given that *DSM-IV* (American Psychiatric Association, 2002) provides five different categories of dissociation. These categories involve disruption of normal cognitive functioning. Two of these categories relate to the issues we have been discussing. The first is dissociative amnesia, where the individual is unable to recall important events from the past that invariably involve traumatic experiences. If guided imagery is recovering the memory then it is undoing the process of dissociation rather than causing it; the problem being whether the client and/or the counsellor can 'handle' the revelation. The second category is depersonalisation disorder, which involves a sense of detachment from thoughts, feelings and bodily experience. Most people report having had experiences of this nature at some time and only when the experience is extreme is it defined as a mental disorder. Individuals engaged in meditation, relaxation and guided imagery will often report a mild experience of this nature and there is no reason to regard this as problematic. The sense of detachment in these situations is often described as pleasurable.

We have had no experience of a client or individual in a training group dissociating in a harmful way during guided imagery and this is after a substantial number of clients and groups who have been through the process over a number of years. Some individuals have become deeply relaxed and have resisted coming out of the relaxed state, but this is because being relaxed is a pleasurable and sometimes novel experience and they want to savour it, rather than hurry back to their more 'normal' state of mind.

We have had one report from a colleague who was helping a client to relax using elements of imagery who did go into a strange state. She presented with high levels of anxiety and panic attacks and was contracted for six sessions. On the second full session she was offered relaxation with imagery with a view to helping her to relax and develop strategies for recognising and controlling her anxiety.

> *Counsellor*: Be aware of your feet on the floor, hands on your thighs and the weight of your body on the sofa. Close your eyes, if it's comfortable. Take a couple of deep breaths and as you breathe out, let go of any tension stored in your body. Allow your breathing to settle to its normal pattern. Let the muscles around your eyes relax. Let the muscles around your mouth relax and allow your tongue to rest in the floor of your mouth. Allow your shoulders to drop and be aware of how it feels to be physically relaxed. Now imagine a time when you felt relaxed and peaceful.

At this point the client opened her eyes and said she couldn't think of one. After a few minutes, she remembered a weekend sitting in her garden chair reading. She had become engrossed in her book and lost track of time. Once she recalled this, she was happy to continue. The relaxation was repeated and then:

> *Counsellor*: Imagine yourself sitting in the garden reading. What's the weather like? What can you hear? Now think of a colour or object that would symbolise the way you feel.
> *Client*: Green.
> *Counsellor*: Where in your body do you feel the most relaxed?
> *Client*: The base of my spine.

The intention was to use the image of the green colour at the base of the spine, and encourage her to breathe into it and spread the feeling of relaxation throughout her body. But she suddenly opened her eyes, looking pale and clammy (it was a hot, humid day) and said she felt faint. The session was halted and she was given a drink of water and asked conversational questions like, what colour was her shirt and who was dog-sitting for her. She felt shaky at this point.

When the client calmed down she described herself as feeling 'floaty' and felt she had been deeply hypnotised. She felt extremely small as if she was floating away towards something black and dense and everything felt closed in and small; hands, feet, legs, arms. She was not aware of having experienced this feeling before and described it as quite pleasant. This level of relaxation was new for her and asked to repeat the exercise. She ascribed the fainting sensation to having had a busy day and the heat and humidity. The session ran 30 minutes over time to ensure the client was fully restored and safe to drive.

The episode was taken to supervision and it was decided that the client had temporarily 'lost her ground' or disassociated. The supervisor felt that this might have been too powerful an exercise for her at that point and advised avoiding relaxation and imagery work in the short term. The client's therapy continued for a further six weeks and the client made considerable progress, recognising that her drinking and lifestyle were still aspects of her difficulties. She thought she would probably return to therapy in the future.

The client was contacted six weeks after the close of therapy and asked if her experience could be used as material for this book. She was happy to give consent and repeated that it hadn't been an unpleasant experience; just a very different one for her, which had probably phased her at the time.

> *Client*:   It's magic really because I still use the image when I can't sleep and
>   have successfully overcome insomnia by visualising the colour green. I
>   had tried tapes before without success. I feel this worked because it
>   came from my own experience, rather than someone else telling me
>   what should be relaxing.

We have included this account as it illustrates two important points.

1   What superficially appears to be risky can turn out to be benign or even thera-
    peutic when the use of imagery is involved. We have had a number of reports
    where the outcome of the imagery experience initially appeared to be negative,
    unpleasant or leaving the client feeling in a 'stuck place', but later, the clients
    themselves reported that the experience had been a beneficial and growthful
    one. In relation to the overall number of positive, enthusiastic responses, the
    number of experiences that clients initially report as negative is tiny. We still have
    no report of the use of metaphoric guided imagery being damaging in the long
    term either from our own practice or the existing literature.
2   The image was drawn from the client's own experience. Here the client is spon-
    taneously supporting our contention that the most effective imagery is self-
    generated. This may indicate a built-in psychological safety cut out mechanism
    which enables the client to control the process in some way.

Here we give a written account provided by a client for whom the initial experience could be misinterpreted as negative but for whom the process was in fact beneficial.

> I was visualising a bird in a cage. I had to describe the cage and become the cage
> and see how it felt. It was strange because I realised that although the cage was a
> restrictive thing to have around the bird, when I was 'being' the cage it felt a very
> safe thing. It was a defence mechanism that I was used to. I was asked to visualise
> whether the bird would leave the cage. I could visualise the bird hopping out of the
> cage, but as the bird came out of the cage, I had the most intense feeling of being

exposed. I became very upset. I started criticising the bird, then the cage and then the visualisation. I couldn't imagine what the bird would do outside the cage. I couldn't allow it to fly; couldn't even imagine the bird getting off the ground.

This was my first time at visualising. I really gave myself the freedom to be creative and picture my feelings, but the strange thing is that this picture became very powerful for me. Later on in the therapy I went back to this picture of the bird. It stayed with me as a theme. I realised one day that I had made progress because I could imagine the bird getting off the ground and flying. The image just came into my head. And I realised that the image of the bird became a way of picturing change and some hope of recovery.

These reports demonstrate that the clients used imagery to confront difficult or negative patterns in their lives in creative meaningful ways. These important images brought the dysfunctional patterns into awareness with a clarity that may not have occurred as a result of verbal interaction.

It is unnecessary for the counsellor to bring a session to a neat conclusion, which may be providing closure to the learning process. We have provided several examples where the client has gained insights some time after the imagery was generated. Being emotionally upset is not necessarily a 'bad' or negative experience, as most counsellors will agree. A client feeling emotionally stirred up is not uncommon and at the end of a 50-minute session the normal practice is to end the session, irrespective of the client's emotional state. There is no way of knowing what the client is walking away with emotionally following any form of therapy. A level of risk is inevitable in all forms of therapeutic work because clients are often in emotionally fragile states and come because they have real difficulties in coping with their lives. As Jersild (1955: 93) reminds us:

It is true that often, as a person enquires into the meaning of his life he is likely to feel uncomfortable. He will find that he has been pretending. He will face feelings that are disturbing and depressing. But these conditions were there before he started to inquire. . . . The search for meaning – the search for selfhood – is painful, and although it is healing, the person who undertakes it is likely to feel worse before he feels better. It is only by accepting oneself as one is . . . that the process of healing and repair can get under way.

Ethical considerations

All therapists welcome ethical guidelines for practice, such as those provided by the accrediting bodies, for example, the British Association for Counselling and Psychotherapy (BACP, 2002). The values, ethical principles, frameworks and personal moral qualities they stipulate are essential and apply to the use of all therapeutic interventions, including imagery work. In this section, we outline the ethical issues that we feel impact specifically on the use of guided imagery work.

It is paramount that counsellors who use guided imagery in practice should receive adequate training and be able to perform at a high level of competence. We know of counselling training courses which do not expose their trainees to any form of imagery experience and make a professional judgement that it is an inappropriate form of counsellor intervention. We would not agree and regard the use of guided imagery and other types of imagery work as important tools for any professional therapist. We recommend a training format in which an experienced imagery guide demonstrates the use of techniques experientially with trainees and then allows an extended and critical discussion with the group. Techniques can then be rehearsed using a dyadic or triadic format, so that each trainee receives detailed feedback on their performance. We also advocate the Interpersonal Process Recall technique designed by Kagan (1984) to help trainees examine non-verbal as well as verbal aspects of their skills development.

As practitioners, the authors have all had elements of guided imagery included in their training and subsequently have set up a three-year research project which involves demonstration, practice, video recording, Interpersonal Process Recall and discussions of the outcomes of working with clients. This research has included the techniques of guided imagery and relaxation described in this book.

A second ethical consideration is the extent to which counsellors meet their own emotional needs rather than those of the client, although this is a risk inherent in all client–counsellor relationships. Most of us have degrees of narcissism and one form of this is to give the impression that, as the counsellor, we are some sort of miracle worker or guru, fostering the client's psychological dependence. Mearns (2003) refers to this as the counsellor's 'need to be clever'. The impact of insights gained from the imagery, even 'aha' moments, can leave clients feeling in awe of the counsellor's skill. If this happens, it is acceptable to acknowledge the client's perception, but to disabuse the client that something miraculous or magical has been done to them. The creative work is done by the client themselves. The counsellor is the experienced guide who only enables the process.

From time to time we have encountered counsellors who may use the client for their own emotional needs and who encourage the client to work through issues that are important to them irrespective of the needs of the client. We have referred to this earlier and it can involve any number of personal issues, such as bereavement, relations with parents, sexual identity and so on. There may be a minority of counsellors who, for their own reasons, have a vested interest in uncovering memories of childhood sexual abuse. However this is a matter of common professional concern and does not refer to the practice of guiding imagery alone.

Issues of transference and countertransference are complex in the use of guided imagery, because the imagery is interposed between the client and the counsellor. However, intuitive feelings about the counsellor, particularly in relation to trustworthiness, will play an important part in the client's willingness to engage with the process, particularly with clients who are suspicious of the counsellor's motives. A more common transference effect is the positive feelings that are generated by the client when they have experienced a deeper state of relaxation and this feeling tends to remain at the end of an imagery journey. This can lead to the belief that the counsellor is all seeing and all knowing and the client denies responsibility for their own learning, maintaining a dependent relationship.

An interesting inclusion in the BACP Ethical Framework (2002) is the moral quality of courage; the capacity to act in spite of known fears, risks and uncertainty. Guiding a client on an imagery journey is a journey into the unknown in that it is far less predictable and controllable than a verbal interaction. Imagery themes might emerge that appear to the novice as risky to explore, particularly where the client appears in imagination to be in physical danger. We have already suggested that if there is a sense that when a situation in a guided imagery journey appears to be risky, it may be an indication that the counsellor should press forward rather than retreat because this can lead to a breakthrough or insight in the client's own work.

There will always be individuals who become accredited in spite of their own shortcomings and this is also true of therapy. Professional bodies exist to monitor the possibility of exploitative, abusive and incompetent practice and to deal with complaints. It is the responsibility of the facilitators of training courses, managers of employing agencies, supervisors and therapists themselves to guarantee professional standards.

Postscript

Imagery techniques are integrated into almost all schools of psychotherapy . . .

(Arbuthnot et al., 2001: 123)

It may be correct to assert that imagery techniques are integrated in theory, but they have by no means been integrated into professional practice. There are still a significant number of training courses in the UK where imagery work of whatever type does not feature on the basic counselling training curriculum. There is even a small but vocal minority of therapists who would have us believe that imagery work is dangerous or damaging to clients. We do not share this belief but we respect the genuine concern which gives rise to it. Imagery techniques, like any other, can be potentially harmful in the hands of an incompetent practitioner. Our ambition is to add to the existing literature using our research, both empirical and literature-based, alongside practical description of how to apply imagery techniques in order to add to the skills base of practitioners.

The theoretical models of counselling and psychotherapy that most closely relate to the processes we have been discussing in this book are Psychosynthesis, Gestalt Therapy and Person-Centred Counselling, but we have shown how it has its place in both psychoanalytic and psychodynamic traditions also. Counsellors and psychotherapists are increasingly willing to incorporate techniques from other models if they find them effective, whether they describe themselves as integrative or eclectic.

The relationship between the use of the imagery techniques and Person-Centred Counselling is complex, because each person-centred counsellor will interpret the model in their own way. Some person-centred counsellors will introduce experiential exercises and activities into their work with clients, whereas others would regard the introduction of structures as directive and therefore interfering with the self-actualising tendency of the client. We would argue that the use of guided imagery as an intervention in itself is self-actualising as it invites the client to explore an often untapped and vast area of experience of their 'being in the world'. We would also expect that the imagery guide possesses the capacity for deep empathic responding or rapport alongside a profound respect for the client's experience in line with Rogers' (1957) core conditions. We would regard ourselves when guiding as being directive or structured in terms of process, but always person-centred in relation to the way we work with the material produced by the client. This is reflected in the guidelines we have provided here. These guidelines are designed to reduce the possibility of manipulating the client and maintaining the client's control of the therapeutic process.

The use of imagery techniques to enhance personal learning goes well beyond the therapeutic couch. They have been successfully incorporated into sport, medicine, personal growth and development courses for adults, personal and social education in schools and many other applications. Research and practice demonstrate positive responses to guided imagery from individuals across a wide range of cultures. In training settings, we have worked with students from a number of African countries, the Americas, most of Europe, South East Asia, including India, China and Indonesia, the Caribbean, Iceland, Australia, Iran, Pakistan and Russia. We have recently had moving accounts from two Jordanian women who used guided imagery in their work with Palestinian children in refugee camps. These positive responses cut across culture, social class and IQ as identified by teachers working in independent and inner-city schools, with both high achieving students and students with special educational needs. One teacher reported using guided imagery successfully with visually handicapped students, including those who had had no sight from birth.

We have purposely foregrounded the voices and experiences of clients and trainees we have worked with over the years. Once again we would like to thank them for their generosity in allowing us to use their material in this book and hope that we have done them justice. We end as we began with the voice of the client. This extract was taken from a student's learning journal, written following a personal development module. He movingly records the impact of how he learned to use his spontaneously occurring imagery in his own personal growth.

I found Eric's comments about imagery very insightful. Often my dreams, daydreams reveal much about what's going on in my head. As long as I had lived I had often gone into very dramatic visualisation, but had never really observed them. They usually involved reactions of parents and my friends to my suicide, a climbing accident, or in a situation where I acted aggressively to deal with a situation – often in violence. I began to observe these images as they occurred. It seemed they reflected a need for sympathy, attention, love, someone to blame. I would sometimes be in tears myself over these visualisations, and often wallowed in them. The aggressive visualisations often reflected my need for justice in the often violent actions my stepfather dealt out to me, and the fact that no one did anything about it. I think to this day, I have still not put that aggressively angry side behind me.

I have observed these images since the course, and have found it a useful exercise to stop the visualisations immediately if they are negative, just as in positive thinking it is useful to observe your thoughts and actions. Observing them also gives me greater insight into what is actually going on in my life, and I believe they are powerful tools to living in an authentic manner. I have been getting into daydreaming positive things instead. Ultimately, the aim is not to dream, but to act, as in the following quote:

All men dream: but not equally. Those who dream by night in the dusty recesses of their minds wake in the day to find it was vanity: but the dreamers of the day are dangerous men, for they act their dreams with open eyes, to make it possible. This I did. (T.E. Lawrence)

References

Achterberg, J. (1985) *Imagery in Healing: Shamanism and Modern Medicine*, Boston: Shambhala.

Aggleton, J.P. (ed.) (1992) *The Amygdala: Neurobiological Aspects of Emotion, Memory and Mental Dysfunction*, New York: Wiley.

American Psychiatric Association (2002) *Diagnostic and Statistical Manual of Mental Disorders*, (4th edn), Washington, DC: American Psychiatric Association.

Arbuthnot, K.D., Arbuthnot, D.W. and Rossiter, L. (2001) 'Guided imagery and memory: implications for psychotherapists', *Journal of Counselling Psychology*, 48(2): 123–32.

Assagioli, R. (1965) *Psychosynthesis: A Manual of Principles and Techniques*, London: Turnstone.

Bachélard, G. (1971) *On Poetic Imagination and Reverie*, New York: Bobbs-Merrill.

Binswanger, L. (1946) 'Über die daseinanalytiche Forschungsrichtung in der Psychiatrie', *Schweizer Archiv für Naurologie und Psychiatrie*, 57: 209–25.

Blofeld, J. (1970) *The Tantric Mysticism of Tibet*, New York: Dutton.

Boss, M. (1963) *Psychoanalysis and Daseinanalysis* (trans. L.B. Lefebre), New York: Basic Books.

Breuer, J. and Freud, S. (1955) 'Studies on hysteria', in J. Strachey (ed.), *The Standard Edition*, Vols 4 and 5, London: Hogarth.

Brigham, D.D. (1994) *Imagery for Getting Well*, New York: Norton.

British Association for Counselling and Psychotherapy (2002) *Ethical Framework for Good Practice in Counselling and Psychotherapy*, Rugby: BACP.

British Psychological Society (1995) *Report on Recovered Memories*, Leicester: British Psychological Society.

Buber, M. (1947) *I and Thou*, Edinburgh: Clark.

Burkitt, E. (2004) 'Drawing conclusions from children's art', *The Psychologist*, 17(10): 566–8.

Caslant, E. (1921) *Méthode de Dévelopment des Facultés Supranormales*, Paris: Edition Rhea.

Courtois, C.A. (2001) 'Commentary on "guided imagery and memory" additional considerations', *Journal of Counselling Psychology*, 48(2): 133–5.

Desoille, R. (1938) *Exploration de l'Affectivite Subconsciente par la Methode de Rêve Éveillé*, Paris: D'Autry.

Desoille, R. (1966) *The Directed Daydream*, New York: Psychosynthesis Foundation.

Ellenberger, H.F. (1970) *The Discovery of the Unconscious*, New York: Basic Books.

Ellis, D. and Cromby, J. (2004) 'It's not always good to talk', *The Psychologist*, 17(11): 630–1.

Enns, C.Z. (2001) 'Some reflections on imagery and psychotherapy implications', *Journal of Counselling Psychology*, 48(2): 136–9.

Ferguson, M. (1983) *The Aquarian Conspiracy: Personal and Social Transformation in the 1980s*, London: Palladin.

Ferrucci, P. (1982) *What We May Be*, Wellingborough: Turnstone Press.

Frank, L. (1910) *Die Psychoanalyse*, Munich: Reinhart.

Frétigny, R. and Virel, A. (1968) *L'Imagerie Mentale*, Geneva: Mont Blanc.

Freud, S. (1900) 'The interpretation of dreams', in J. Strachey (ed.) (1962) *The Standard Edition*, Vols 4 and 5, London: Hogarth.

Fromm, E. (1951) *The Forgotten Language*, New York: Rinehart.

Galton, F. (1883) *Inquiries into Human Faculty and its Development*, London: Dent.

Gerard, R. (1964) *Psychosynthesis: A Psychotherapy for the Whole Man*, 14. New York: Psychosynthesis Research Foundation.

Gerard, R. (1967) 'Symbolic identification: a technique of psychosynthesis', *Acta Medica*: 710–1.

Graham, H. (1990) *Time, Energy and the Psychology of Healing*, London: Jessica Kingsley.

Grinder, J. and Bandler, R. (1981) *Trance-formations*, Moab, UT: Real People Press.

Hall, E. (1983) 'Patterns of meaning in guided fantasy', *Journal of Mental Imagery*, 7(1): 35–50.

Hall, E. (1999) 'Four noble truths for counselling', in G. Watson, S. Batchelor and G. Claxton (eds), *The Psychology of Awakening: Buddhism, Science and Our Day-to-Day Lives*, London: Rider.

Hall, E. and Greenwood, E. (1986) 'The effects of fantasy on the expression of feeling and quality of writing in young adolescents', in D.G. Russell, D.F. Marks and T.E. Richardson (eds), *Imagery 2*, Dunedin, New Zealand: Human Performance Associates.

Hall, E. and Hall, C. (1988) *Human Relations in Education*, London: Routledge.

Hall, E. and Kirkland, A. (1984) 'Drawings of trees and the expression of feelings in early adolescence', *British Journal of Guidance and Counselling*, 7(1): 39–45.

Hall, E., Hall, C. and Leech, A. (1990) *Scripted Fantasy in the Classroom*, London: Routledge.

Hall, E., Hall, C. and Sirin, A. (1996) 'Professional and personal development for teachers: the application of learning following a counselling module', *British Journal of Educational Psychology*, 66: 383–98.

Happich, C. (1932) 'Das Bildewusstein als ansatzstelle psychischer Behandlung', *Zentreblatt Psychotherapie*, 5.

Heinschel, J.A. (2002) 'A descriptive study of the Interactive Guided Imagery experience', *Journal of Holistic Nursing*, 20(4): 325–46.

Hornby, G., Hall, C. and Hall, E. (2003) *Counselling Pupils in Schools: Skills and Strategies*, London: Routledge Falmer.

Hume, D. (1912) *An Inquiry Concerning Human Nature*, Chicago: Open Court.

Ignatius, of Lyola Saint (1992) *The Spiritual Exercises of Saint Ignatius Lyola; a Translations and Commentary* (trans. George E. Gauss), Chicago: Lyola Press.

Jersild, A.T. (1955) *When Teachers Face Themselves*, New York: Teacher's College, Columbia University.

Joyce, B.R. (1984) 'Dynamic disequilibrium: the intelligence of growth', *Theory into Practice*, 23(1): 26–34.

Jung, C.G. (1959) 'Archetypes and the collective uncounscious', in *The Collected Works of C.G. Jung*, Vol. 9, London: Routledge and Kegan Paul.

Jung, C.G. (1960) 'The transcendent function', in *The Collected Works of C.G. Jung*, Vol. 8, London: Routledge and Kegan Paul.

Jung, C.G. (1961) *Memories, Dreams and Reflections* (ed. Aniela Jaffe), New York: Random House.

Kagan, N. (1984) 'Interpersonal process recall: basic methods and recent research', in D. Larson (ed.), *Teaching Psychological Skills: Models for giving Psychology Away*, Monterey, CA: Brooks/Cole.

Kaplan, E.K. (1972) 'Gaston Bachélard's philosophy of imagination: an introduction', *Phenomenological Research*, 33: 1–24.

Kelley, C.R. (1974) *Education in Feeling and Purpose*, Santa Monica, CA: The Radix Institute.

Kelly, G. (1955) *The Psychology of Personal Constructs*, Vol. 1, New York: Norton.

Kretschmer, W. (1969) 'Meditative techniques in psychotherapy', in C. Tart (ed.), *Altered States of Consciousness*, New York: Wiley.

Leuner, H. (1969) 'Guided affected imagery (GIA): a method of intensive therapy', *American Journal of Psychotherapy*, 23(1): 4–22.

Leuner, H. (1984) *Guided Affective Imagery: Mental Imagery in Short-Term Psychotherapy*, New York: Thieme-Stratton.

Leuner, H., Horn, G. and Klessman, E. (1983) *Guided Affective Imagery with Children and Adolescents*, New York: Plenum.

Lowen, A. (1975) *Bioenergetics*, New York: Coward.

Mahrer, A.R. and Nadler, W.P. (1986) 'Good moments in psychotherapy: a preliminary review, a list and some promising research avenues', *Journal of Consulting and Clinical Psychology*, 54(1): 10–15.

Mason, J.L. (2001) *Guide to Stress Reduction*, Berkeley, CA: Celestial Arts.

McLeod, J. (2003) *Doing Counselling Research* (2nd edn), London: Sage.

Mearns, D. (2003) *Developing Person-centred Counselling* (2nd edn), London: Sage.

Moreno, J.L. (1967) 'Reflections on my method of group psychotherapy and psychodrama', in H. Greenwald (ed.), *Active Psychotherapy*, New York: Atherton.

Myers, F. (1885) 'Automatic writing', *Proceedings of the Society for Psychical Research*, 3: 1–63.

Naparstek, B. (1995) *Staying Well with Guided Imagery*, London: Thorsons.

O'Connell, A. and O'Connell, V.F. (1974) *Choice and Change: An Introduction to the Psychology of Growth*, Englewood Cliffs, NJ: Prentice Hall.

Owen, I.R. (1991) 'Using the sixth sense: the place and relevance of language in counselling', *British Journal of Guidance and Counselling*, 19(3): 307–19.

Perky, C.W. (1910) 'An experimental study of imagination', *American Journal of Psychology*, 21: 422–52.

Perls, F.S. (1969) *Gestalt Therapy Verbatim*, Moab, UT: Real People Press.

Perls, F.S. (1973) *The Gestalt Approach and Eye Witness to Therapy*, Palo Alto, CA: Science and Behaviour Books.

Porter, K. (2003) *The Mental Athlete*, Champaign, IL: Human Kinetics Press.

Pylyshyn, Z.W. (1973) 'What the mind's eye tells the mind's brain: a critique of mental imagery', *Psychological Bulletin*, 80(1): 1–23.

Rasmussen, S. (2004) 'The imperfection of perfectionism', *The Psychologist*, 17(7): 398–400.

Reich, W. (1949) *Character Analysis*, New York: Noonday.

Richardson, A. (1969) *Mental Imagery*, London: Routledge and Kegan Paul.

Roe, A. (1951) 'A study of imagery in research scientists', *Journal of Personality*, 19: 459–470.

Rogers, C.R. (1951) *Client-Centered Therapy*, Boston: Houghton Mifflin.

Rogers, C.R. (1957) 'The necessary and sufficient conditions of therapeutic personality change', *Journal of Consulting Psychology*, 21(2): 95–103.

Rowan, J. (1983) *The Reality Game: A Guide to Humanistic Counselling and Therapy*, London: Routledge and Kegan Paul.

Rowan, J. (1990) *Subpersonalities: The People Inside Us*, London: Routledge and Kegan Paul.

Rubin, J.A. (ed.) (2001) *Approaches to Art Therapy: Theory and Technique*, New York: Brunner-Routledge.

Satir, V. (1972) *Peoplemaking*, Palo Alto, CA: Science and Behaviour Books.

Schultz, J.H. and Luthe, W. (1969) *Autogenic Methods*, New York: Grune and Stratton.

Schutz, W.C. (1967) *Joy: Expanding Human Awareness*, New York: Grove Press.

Segal, S.J. and Nathan, S. (1964) 'The Perky effect: incorporation of an external into an imagery experience under placebo and control conditions', *Perceptual and Motor Skills*, 18: 385–95.

Shattock, E.H. (1979) *Mind Your Body*, London: Turnstone.

Short, P.L. (1953) 'The objective study of mental imagery', *British Journal of Psychology*, 44: 38–51.

Simonton, O.C., Matthews-Simonton, S. and Creighton, J.L. (1980) *Getting Well Again*, New York: Bantam Books.

Singer, J. (1966) *Daydreaming*, New York: Random House.

Singer, J. (1974) *Imagery and Daydream Methods in Psychotherapy and Behavior Modification*, New York: Academic Press.

Solms, M. and Turnbull, O. (2002) *The Brain and the Inner World*, London: Karnac.

Springer, S.P. and Deutsch, G. (1998) *Left Brain, Right Brain: Perspectives from Cognitive Neuroscience*, New York: W.H. Freeman.

Stevens, J.O. (1971) *Awareness: Exploring, Experimenting, Experiencing*, Moab, UT: Real People Press.

Thomas, G.V. and Jolley, R.P. (1998) 'Drawing conclusions: a re-examination of empirical and conceptual bases for psychological evaluation of children from their drawings', *British Journal of Clinical Psychology*, 37: 127–39.

Totton, N. (2003) *Body Psychotherapy: An Introduction*, Buckingham: OUP.

Watkins, M.M. (1976) *Waking Dreams*, New York: Interface.

Zohar, D. and Marshall, I. (2000) *Spiritual Intelligence: The Ultimate Intelligence*, London: Bloomsbury.

Index